WEALTH
BEYOND
MONEY

**UNLOCKING
THE 6 DIMENSIONS OF SUCCESS
FOR RICHNESS IN EVERY AREA OF YOUR LIFE**

ETHAN KING

Wealth Beyond Money

Copyright © 2022 by Ethan King

SIMPLE Success Systems LLC
Atlanta, GA.

IISBN 978-0-9856056-3-6 (paperback)
ISBN 978-0-9856056-4-3 (hardcover)

Printed in the United States of America.

DISCLAIMER: No material in this book is intended to be a substitute
for professional medical advice, legal advice, or financial advice. Always
consult your qualified provider with any questions you have, and never
disregard professional advice or delay in seeking it because of something
you read in this book, or on any materials mentioned by the author.

WHAT PEOPLE ARE SAYING

"Ethan King has brought forward some of the most important aspects for all business leaders and entrepreneurs…"
—Dr. Michael Breus, PhD aka "The Sleep Doctor"

"…a cross between a juicy memoir and a highlight reel for cracking the code on life. This book is actionable."
—Darcie Adler, Founder/Creative Director, The Spin Style Agency LLC

"Move over Tony Robbins, Ethan King's *Wealth Beyond Money* is the complete life guide to success."
—Maureen Ryan-Blake, Best-selling Author, TV Show Host, Publisher

"If you 'want it all' read this book… chock full of exercises and pathways you can use to make your road to financial success shorter and easier."
—Vincent M. Roazzi, Best-selling Author of *The Spirituality of Success, Getting Rich with Integrity*

"With a refreshing practical perspective and relatable examples, Ethan's book feels distinctly *real*. It's not theory or concepts…"
—Brad Stevens, Founder/CEO, OutsourceAccess.com

"King's book is a pocket compass. Use it to activate your inner guidance to be a better person, make the right decisions and live your best life."
—Tanya Chernova, Award Winning Speaker, Co-Founder Courageous Living

"…a must-read for all entrepreneurs, whether you are just starting or have been a lifetime entrepreneur like myself."
—Steve Distante, CEO Vanderbilt Financial Group

"…practical, proven wisdom about how to get your mind in a good place."
—Conor Neill, President of Vistage in Spain & Professor at IESE Business School

"For those looking to implement an intentional plan for their life, *Wealth Beyond Money* is a must read."
—John Marshall, Community Builder, ReEngage Now

"…a timely narrative, given society's movement towards greater spiritual and emotional fulfillment…both entertaining and educational… A true must read."
—Samir Damani, MD, PharmD, Founder CEO, iThriveMD

"Living a happy and fulfilled life is everyone's goal, and perhaps the most elusive goal. In this book, Ethan delivers direct access to that kind of life."
—Saurel Quettan, Executive and Leadership Coach, ExeQfit, Inc.

"…an action-packed resource to help me create an abundant, well-rounded life, business, and legacy."
—Cody James Aikin, Host of the Pillars of Freedom Podcast

"…this book helped me re-align with my purpose and put perspective to the pursuit of success."
—Dr. Ivan Salaberrios, President and Founder, AIM Technical Services

"Not only does this provide you with practical tips, it also inspires and motivates you as you are taken on a journey…"
—Heléne Smuts, Founder, Credo Growth

"Truly, this book is a powerful tool that gets one thinking about applying these valuable lessons to one's own scenarios."
—Abeer Qumsieh, Founder and CEO, Better Business

"Ethan's well-written book highlights the most important mental constructs that will serve you extremely well, not just in business but in life overall."
—Samir Patel, Managing Partner, Trophy Point High Yield Income

"… a must-read, not only for up-and-coming entrepreneurs, but for anyone who wants something different in life…"
—Kris Favers, Marketing Professional

"The fundamentals outlined in this book are a great reality check…"
—Dr. Justin Scott, Founder, Pure Dental Health

"…actionable steps to help you on your journey of a successful and fulfilled life."
—Marshall Chiles, Serial Entrepreneur

"…every person who desires well-rounded success should have this book in her library."
— Smita
Indie pop star, TV Host, Entrepreneur, Social Activist
@smitapop

CONTENTS

FOREWORD

I have known Ethan for several years. We are both members of the global Entrepreneurs' Organization (EO) which has some 15,000 CEO members in 70 countries. I am the Dean of Learning for the EO Leadership Academies, which are held all over the world. I have been blessed to have had the opportunity to be CEO of several companies, both public and private, and to have led many large not-for-profits. I have also been able to serve in the White House as Appointments Secretary to the President of the United States.

I first met Ethan during his tenure as EO Chapter President of Atlanta, when he invited me to be the keynote speaker on the subject of "Taking Your Life to the Next Level." The talk is about reaching the next level of your life, based on specific principles, and creating a life by design.

Ethan's theme for the year was EVOLVE, and I remember his Board's mission was to help every member become the best possible version of themselves so that they may help others become the best versions of themselves, as well. I viewed this as a noble mission, and my talk set the stage for some of the other amazing experiences they had during that year. Ethan's leadership was pivotal to broadening the scope of the members' visions for what they could do to influence the lives of others. The quote, "it is not enough to be a good leader, but rather you must be a leader for good," comes to mind as the best example of what the EO Atlanta Chapter determined to do.

A year later, I had the opportunity to spend 5 days with Ethan and 29 other entrepreneurial leaders from around the world at the EO Global Leadership Academy in Washington, D.C., where I got to know Ethan better and learn some of his backstory. As I began to understand his background, I could see what makes him such an effective leader in his own unique way.

There is much to admire about Ethan, his spiritual growth, commitment to health, and business leadership, but what impresses me even more is his commitment to family and his desire to make a contribution to the greater good, to be engaged in a cause greater than self. His knowledge that all that we give into the lives of others comes back into our own, is key to making the greater contribution. His understanding that helping others is our real mission resonates with all of us. Ethan and I share these beliefs and principles, and he is imminently qualified to write this book.

I am writing this foreword as a tribute to Ethan, and all that he stands for, and the way in which he models his life. In my book, *The Leader Within Us*, I speak about the idea that one can have it all. One can enjoy success in family, business, community, and within oneself, if we just find the rhythm and pace that is right for us. Ethan believes that with the right mindset, principles, and tools it is possible for everyone reading this to have it all. If one starts implementing these steps today, one can unlock the potential within oneself and live a holistically abundant life by design.

Wealth Beyond Money demystifies the process and breaks it down into SIMPLE easy-to-remember, actionable steps. It is possible for everyone reading this to have it all in every dimension of life, without sacrificing anything that truly matters.

I recommend this book as a must read without hesitation or equivocation. It has the possibility to truly transform your life.

Warren Rustand
Author of *The Leader Within Us*
Former Appointments Secretary to the President
Former Global Chair of the World Presidents Organization
Dean of Learning for the EO Global Leadership Academy

INTRODUCTION: WHO THIS BOOK IS FOR

For the executive who wants to build a great business and enjoy quality time with family and friends.

For the dreamer who wants an extraordinary life, knowing that you have tons of untapped potential.

For the hungry warrior who unashamedly wants it all, yet has been told that you have to give up something in order to get what you want.

For the adventurer who wants ultimate freedom, unlimited wealth, amazing experiences, and fulfilling relationships throughout the duration of your long, healthy life

For the thinker who considers the phrase "you can't have your cake and eat it too" to be the dumbest saying in the history of humanity, because what good is having a cake if you can't eat it? This book is for you.

No matter where you are in life, you can have it all!

If you throw away the concept of life balance and instead adopt a new way of thinking, which I will teach you in this book, yes *you* can have it all.

In this book, you will learn a fresh and *SIMPLE* framework to replace old notions of life balance so you can achieve extraordinary success in all six dimensions of life, without sacrificing what matters.

Think about the word "balance" for a moment. What comes to mind?

A seesaw? The scales of justice?

The problem with this concept is that the only way for one side to be up, is for the other side to be down. There's no way for both sides to be up at the same time. This would defy the laws of nature. With the constraints of balance, the best thing you can hope for is both sides being average or mediocre.

But what if I told you there was another way?

A way that I have experienced in my life through trial and error, countless hours of research, and studying phenomenal women and men who have come before me and accomplished everything they want in life—and they continue to accomplish more.

This doesn't mean that bad things won't ever happen in your life. As you will read in the coming pages, lots of crazy hardships have happened to me over the years. I've discovered that no matter what, you can still have everything you truly want in life.

I've been robbed, cheated, lied to, vandalized, slandered, and more. I've gone from being broke and buried in debt to richer than I could have ever imagined. But through it all, I have learned to adopt a new mindset that nothing is really *good* or *bad*.

What's equally true: *everything* is both good *and* bad.

This is called The Law of Polarity.

Everything in our universe has a dual nature—up and down, north and south, light and dark. It's like two poles on a magnet. One can't exist without the other.

In the same way, everything that happens to you is both good and bad. It's all a matter of perspective.

> I once heard a fable about a king and his doctor who went out hunting together.
> During the hunting expedition, the king gets a cut on his finger. He says to the doctor, "This is bad! Fix it!"

The doctor refuses to treat the king's finger and simply says "Could be bad, could be good, who knows?"

Weeks later, the king's finger later gets infected and eventually has to be amputated.

After losing his finger, the king is furious with the doctor and has him locked away in a cell. The doctor simply says again, "Could be good, could be bad, who knows?"

More time passes, and the king goes out hunting again, but this time he is alone because the doctor is locked away. The king gets ambushed and kidnapped by a neighboring tribe.

The tribe is just about to sacrifice the king, but they stop because, for their god, a sacrifice must be perfect. Since the king only has only nine fingers, he is considered imperfect, and the tribe releases him, unharmed.

The king runs back to his kingdom and thanks the doctor for not treating his finger because if he still had ten fingers, he would be dead now. The king profusely apologizes to the doctor for locking him away.

The doctor replies, "Could be good, could be bad, who knows? If you had not locked me away, I would have been out hunting with you . . . and I have ten fingers."

There are many variations of this story, from different cultures, with different characters, told many different ways over the years, but the moral is still the same: **nothing is good or bad; everything is both good *and* bad.**

This story illustrates the point that nothing is exclusively good or bad.

Choose to believe that everything is happening for your good. If you look at it that way, the scales are always up!

One of the passages most often quoted from Paulo Coelho's bestselling spiritual novel *The Alchemist* reads: "When you want something, all the universe conspires in helping you to achieve it."

Armed with this knowledge, I've become a different kind of conspiracy theorist. I choose to believe everything that happens is a conspiracy to help me achieve what I want. I may not understand it at the time; it may feel painful or appear to be a setback, but I trust that ultimately it is for my good.

> *"And we know that all things work together for good to those who love God, to those who are called according to His purpose."*
> —*Romans 8:28 KJV*

But wait. You might be thinking to yourself, that Bible verse says "according to God's purpose," not *my* purpose. You are 100% correct. The key is getting in alignment with the universe's purpose for you. When your desires and the will of God (or the universe, or whatever you call God) are completely aligned, that's when the magic happens—and keeps happening.

We are made in the image of God. God is a creator, so we are creators too—like little flames from the master flame.

Getting in alignment doesn't mean you have to give up things you want and succumb to the will of some mean, boring god who wants you to live a miserable life. In fact, just the opposite is true. The universe wants a rich and fulfilling life for you.

So how do you get in alignment? This book will show you how. Forget balance. Balance is boring.

Abundance is amazing.

CHAPTER 1:
THE SIMPLE FRAMEWORK

Robert Owen, a Welsh manufacturer and labor activist, developed the notion of splitting the day into three equal sections, "Eight hours labor, eight hours recreation, eight hours rest," in 1817. This was one of the earliest versions of work-life balance, adopted after the Industrial Revolution in England, where the average worker would work sixteen hours a day, six days a week.

For decades since then, society has led us to believe that you have to give up something—that some sort of compromise is required—to have a balanced life.

Have you ever thought to yourself, "If I focus too hard on my career, then my marriage or my health will suffer"?

Or maybe you've thought something like, "Well, I'm not going to focus *too* hard on my fitness and try to get six-pack abs because that would take too much time away from my business and I'll miss opportunities."

Well, what if I told you that you can have it all, and it's more *SIMPLE* than you think?

In this book, I will teach you how to optimize for *abundance* in ALL areas of your life—health, wealth, relationships, and happiness—without having to sacrifice one for the other.

Sound too good to be true? Consider this:

Did you know that the wings of an airplane are not rigid? They are actually continuously in motion.

Airplane wings are made up of smaller components, gears, and flaps that are continuously calibrating for flight conditions—to adjust for gusts of wind, turbulence, and obstacles.

Sometimes the movements of these flaps are tiny and barely noticeable. Other times, the movements are much more dramatic.

In the same way, your life has six areas that need continuous, contextual calibration. The acronym spells the word SIMPLE.

S – Subconscious restructuring. Stillness, spirituality, the Self. Everything in this area relates to your inner game.

I – Intellectual improvement and implementation. Feeding your brain with knowledge, then applying the information you learned.

M – Money mastery, or material wealth. Anything dealing with your business, career, or financial investments falls in this category.

P – Physical presence. Not just health, fitness, and nutrition, but also your outward appearance—the way you groom and dress yourself.

L – Love & leadership. The focus here is on your relationships—with your family, friends, partners, coworkers, and employees.

E – Entertaining experiences. You could have it all in the other five categories yet still be bored out of your mind. It is vitally important to intentionally design or participate in *fun* experiences to create lasting memories.

I refer to these as the 6 Dimensions of Success.

Henry David Thoreau said that "Wealth is the ability to fully experience life." The goal of this book is to help you achieve and maintain *6-dimensional* wealth, by leveling-up every life area.

We will dive deep into each of the dimensions and teach you actionable, SIMPLE micro-adjustments to make so that you can *have it all* along your life journey and reach any and every destination you desire.

I encourage you to study every chapter, even if it's an area in which you think that you are doing well, or if it's an area that you tend to disregard as being unimportant. The fact that you are dismissing it could be a signal that those areas need focus and development in your life. It may feel uncomfortable to face these challenges, but this book will give you the tools you need.

You will learn decision-making frameworks to help you decrease stress and anxiety, increase clarity and productivity, and give you the ability to be fully present.

You'll be able to grow your business exponentially without sacrificing your soul, your health, or your relationships.

After completing this book, you will throw out the old notions of life balance and adopt a new model that brings you ultimate life *abundance*. Because balance is boring, and abundance is amazing!

Let's begin the journey.

YOU ALREADY HAVE A SIX-PACK

In my *6-Pack Mindset* fitness programs, one of the first lessons I teach is that we all have six-pack abs. For most of us, however, our six-pack is just covered up by the fat we've accumulated over the years.

In much the same way, in every area of life, you have the seeds of potential already inside of you. You just need the tools, mindset, and actions to uncover these dormant qualities, burn away the excess fat—the useless stuff that really doesn't matter—and live the life of your dreams.

CHAPTER 2:
THE GUIDING PRINCIPLES

There are 5 guiding principles that are the foundation for everything else in this book.

PRINCIPLE #1: ELIMINATE THE LUKEWARM

"If it's not a hell yes, it's a no."
—Derek Sivers, founder of CD Baby

Try to edit everything in your life, down to the things that you are either "hot" (passionately excited) about or "cold" (not excited at all) about. Get rid of everything that you are only "lukewarm" (ambivalent) about.

Forget about what opinions people might have of you; this is your one life that you get to live. Life is like a board game, and you only get one journey around the board. So why live it seeking acceptance from others? Live life on your own terms.

For example, I used to watch professional sports, like football and basketball on TV, but as I got older I realized that watching sports only brought me a small amount of joy. So I stopped watching them altogether. I know, as anti-American as that sounds, just understand that that's what works for *my* life. Giving up watching professional sports had absolutely no negative impact on my life, other than making small talk kind of awkward in some social environments, when someone assumes

I am up on the latest developments in the sports world and they make a reference that I don't understand. In situations like this, I reply with a fake emotional response that just agrees with their demeanor, then I quickly change the subject. Or if they persist, I just honestly tell them that I missed the game, but what they are describing sounds awesome.

So that's how I can still have it all, because "all" is everything I care about. For you, giving up sports may be a non-negotiable, and that's perfectly fine.

I also cut the cord on cable TV over a decade ago. Even though I have flat screen TVs throughout my house, they are mostly there for decoration because I don't even have TV programming. Don't get me wrong, I do still have certain premium apps like Netflix, Disney and HBO, but that's it. I found that having 200 cable channels that I wasn't even watching was a complete waste of money, so I put it out of my life altogether. It's either hell yeah or no, so I decided it was a no.

When it comes to food, back in 2012, I read a book called *Wheat Belly* that describes all of the harmful effects of modern-day processed gluten. So for a three-week experiment, I decided to give up all gluten and see how it impacted my health. I lost about twenty pounds and my brain felt clearer than ever. I also noticed that my complexion started to look better, and it felt like my thinning hair started to regrow. I don't know if that was causation or correlation, but for me, all of those benefits felt much better than eating bread. I don't miss bread at all, so I didn't feel like I was giving up anything. Actually, I did miss drinking beer a little bit, but even that craving subsided after a while. I still occasionally drink liquor and wine, I just don't drink beer anymore because of the gluten. But again, that's me. That's what works for my life. You have to figure out what your "maybes" are and just get rid of them.

I also used to read comic books and play video games, but I cut that out too because, after a while, those things were replaced with other interests. Things will change in your life. Something that used to bring you massive enjoyment will eventually seem blasé.

You need to acknowledge Commitment and Consistency Bias: people's strong desire to be, and to appear, consistent with what they have done in the past. You might keep doing something even though it doesn't bring you the same amount of joy anymore. Once you recognize consistency bias happening, just cut out the habit and let it go so you can make more room for new things that are a "hell yeah."

The exception to this rule is when it comes to honoring others. Don't skip your mother's eightieth birthday party simply because it might be boring for you. If someone is important to you, honor him or her. That should be a "hell yeah" for you.

PRINCIPLE #2: IF SOMEONE ELSE HAS DONE IT, I COULD DO IT

A mentee of mine once asked me about my diet for staying lean, and I explained to him that when I really want to cut weight, I go on a *no-beige diet*, meaning I avoid all beige-colored foods like chips, fried foods, bagels, donuts, rice, cereal, potatoes, etc., and instead focus on a colorful palette of grilled or baked meats, fish, leafy greens, fruits, and vegetables. This is an intensified version of my gluten-free diet described above. His response to me was, "That's impossible."

I thought to myself, and would say to him later, "It's not impossible. I just told you that I did it. So if I can do it, just about anyone can do it."

There's nothing that special about me, or anyone else on this Earth. We all breathe oxygen and bleed red blood.

A core belief of mine is that if someone else has done something, *and my desire is strong enough*, I can learn how to do it too.

Some might argue that heredity, physical makeup, and innate talent play a part in our capabilities. While that is sometimes a valid argument, it can also just be an excuse.

For example, let's say I really, really wanted to be a professional basketball player. The first thing I would do is look up other professional NBA players who are similar in height and weight to me. It turns out there have been ten NBA players my height (5'8") or shorter.[1] So that eliminates the physical excuse.

Now I would just need to study their game, hire a great coach, and devote a life of practice to the craft. And I would need tons of hard work and practice because I really, really suck at basketball.

Of course, this all hinges on strong desire. If your desire is genuine and strong enough, let nothing stop you from achieving your goal. Study the greats to fill the knowledge gap, then outwork everyone else to fill the talent gap.

The key is to look for examples of people like you who have succeeded where you want to succeed. When you constantly seek out positive examples instead of negative examples, then soon, all you see is the positive examples. Just like the same way that when you buy a new car, you start to notice that same car everywhere. This phenomenon occurs because of the reticular activating system (RAS) in our brain. The RAS is a cluster of neurons that helps your brain build connections and remember things. You can retrain your brain filter out the negative reinforcements so that

---

[1] Yash Matange, "Who are the 10 shortest players in NBA history?" *NBA.com*, September 15, 2021, https://ca.nba.com/news/who-are-10-shortest-players-nba-history-mugsy-bogues-spud-webb-boykins/zjapq718gzek16uxepv5w284r

you only really notice the positive instances of what you want in life.[2] More on this later.

PRINCIPLE #3: THINK "AND" INSTEAD OF "EITHER/ OR"

Whenever you're faced with a situation in which you want two things, but you feel like you have to give up one for the other, think again. Be resourceful.

One time, I had a big opportunity to speak at a conference in another city, but the next morning my son had a big soccer game. Of course, I could have flown back immediately after my speech, but I also wanted to attend the rest of the conference and the dinners and the afterparties. I also genuinely wanted to be at his soccer game. They were both a "hell yeah" for me.

So I did the speech, which went well, attended the rest of the conference and met some awesome entrepreneurs, partied all night, and went straight to the airport for a six a.m. flight.

As soon as I landed back in Atlanta, I went straight to my son's soccer game and saw him score three goals against the opposing team. Their team won the last season of the game, and he was the MVP!

I was able to pull this off because when situations like this occur, I naturally think "how can I do both?" instead of giving one thing up for the other.

---

[2] Livvie Brault, "Your Brain Filters Out Information That Contradicts Your Beliefs — But You Can Reprogram It," *Your Tango*, July 3, 2021, https://www.yourtango.com/self/how-to-train-reticular-activating-system-keep-open-mind

PRINCIPLE #4: ATTRACT, DON'T CHASE

"Whatever you chase will run away from you. So, stop chasing success and realize you already have it all."
—*Russell Simmons*

Lessons I've learned the hard way:

Someone chasing a relationship comes across as desperate, and it is a turn off. Instead, become the ideal mate of the type of person you seek, and that person will be attracted to you.

Someone chasing money will likely find it hard to get and keep money for long periods of time. If you want to be a wealthy CEO, first start thinking and behaving like one. Study what they study, walk how they walk, talk how they talk. The money and success you desire will come to you.

Someone chasing physical fitness might work out for a few weeks then quit. If you want to be in amazing physical shape, become a runner and bodybuilder in your mind first. Think how they think, do what they do, eat what they eat. Become that person first, then the body of your dreams will be attracted to you.

First become the person that you need to be, and then the things that you want in life will be attracted to you. But if you chase them, they will elude you.

PRINCIPLE #5: THERE ARE NO RULES.

> *"Life can be much broader once you discover one simple fact: Everything around you that you call life was made up by people that were no smarter than you. And you can change it, you can influence it. . . Once you learn that, you'll never be the same again."*
> —Steve Jobs

The things we call rules were just made up by people who came before us who were trying to figure stuff out just like we are. These rules and constraints that we have on us were created by our parents, and their parents, and their parents, who at one point were just kids trying to figure it out too.

I'm not advocating for you to break the law. I'm saying don't feel constrained by cultural rules, traditions, and expectations. It's all made up, and you can live life on your own terms.

CHAPTER 3:
MISALIGNMENT

*"What the universe will manifest when you are in alignment with
it is a lot more interesting than what you try to manifest."*
—Adyashanti

I was nineteen years old, sitting alone in a cold jail cell, crying uncontrollably. I had just hung up the phone with my dad, who said to me "This is the last time, Ethan. If this happens again, I'm not bailing you out. You'll have to stay in there."

As the tears streamed down my face, all I could think to myself was, "I'm such a disappointment."

How did I get here?

To answer that question, we have to go a little further back into my childhood.

From an early age, I knew I wanted to be an artist. I was really into drawing and painting, and in high school I even had my work in exhibitions. When I told my parents that I wanted to pursue art as a career, they said, "Artists only make money after they're dead."

My parents wanted the best for me, and I think they knew that I secretly wanted to be rich. It's not that I grew up poor—if I had to guess, we were middle class—but we never had family conversations about money, and my mom was extremely frugal, so I *felt* poor. It seemed like my friends could get whatever they wanted, but I was usually told *no*.

Later, I would learn that I was very blessed, but from the warped perspective of a kid with limited information, I was unappreciative.

My mom worked long hours. I recall her sometimes making comments like, "Money doesn't grow on trees" or "Some people think money just comes out of thin air, but it doesn't."

Every Sunday, we attended Sunday School and church, where I was indoctrinated with verses like "The love of money is the root of all evil" and "It is easier for a camel to go through the eye of a needle than for someone who is rich to enter the kingdom of God."

Because of the combination of these things, I felt like we didn't have much money, but that that was actually a *good* thing because if we did, we would go to hell.

Deep inside, something about this concept just never made sense to me. Why would God want us to be poor?

I remember watching shows like *Lifestyles of the Rich and Famous*, and thinking to myself, "I want to live like that," then feeling bad for even having the thought.

So the moment I moved out of my parents' house at age seventeen, I never looked back.

The summer after my freshman year in college, I moved into an apartment with my friends (against my parents' will) and bought my own car, an eight-year-old Cadillac that I financed for $4,000, even though the *check engine* light was on when I bought it.

I wanted freedom and independence more than anything else. I wanted to do things my way. The problem was, I couldn't afford the life-style I desired, so I hustled by any means necessary—legal or illegal—to get money.

I did everything from petty theft to credit card fraud, from check fraud to selling weed. The first time I got arrested was for *intent to shoplift*, which I didn't even know was a crime.

My punishment was community service, which unfortunately wasn't enough to change my behavior. To be honest, I was probably influenced by too many gangster movies and too much gangsta rap music. These gangsta rap lyrics rang loud in my brain, and I was misguided.

The second time I got arrested was for stealing textbooks from one store and selling them back to a different store off campus. I kept this up for a whole summer and made thousands of dollars, all of which was blown on new clothes and wild nights out in Atlanta.

I soon learned, though, that the criminal life wasn't for me because I have a very recognizable face. The bookstore clerks called the police after realizing that I was returning books very frequently and writing a different name on the return slip each time.

So there I was, back in jail. Crying. Scared.

When I got out, my dad said something that should have been very obvious to me, but I had to learn it the hard way: "Ethan, life is a lot easier when you're a law-abiding citizen."

An easy life is what I actually wanted, but through my actions, I was making a hard life for myself. I was misaligned. So I decided that was the end of my criminal career. But that was far from the end of my troubles.

The president of the university at the time, Michael Adams, summoned me to his office and suspended me for one semester. I'm lucky I wasn't expelled.

I also paid back every single penny that was stolen.

Now that my transgressions were behind me, I just wanted to hurry up and finish school. I worked a few odd jobs but couldn't make any real money while I was still in school because I had to go to class and study. I remember once working as a museum security guard, earning $4.70 per hour. I couldn't wait to graduate and start earning some real money, or so I thought.

Before I graduated, I pledged a fraternity—Kappa Alpha Psi—because the fraternity's ideals really resonated with me: *Achievement in every field of human endeavor.* I was also intrigued by the fact that there are no honorary members of Kappa Alpha Psi. Everyone, no matter how rich or famous, had to earn his place in our Noble Clan.

My zeal for my fraternity, combined with my artistic talent, led me to designing our chapter flyers, t-shirts, and jackets. Soon, other Greek organizations on campus hired me to design their promotional gear too.

As a school project in one of my Digital Multimedia classes, we had to create a fictitious company and build the website and all of the brand materials for that company. So I bought the domain name stuff-4GREEKS.com and launched my project—a fictitious company that offered design services for Greek-letter organizations. This was around the year 2000, when the world wide web was still in its infancy. Upon completion of the class project, I just let the site remain there out on the public web. More on this later.

After graduating from college, I found it difficult to find steady employment. It probably didn't help that I only had an art degree and a not-so-clean criminal record. Some nights, I was so hungry that all I had for dinner was microwave popcorn. I was literally a starving artist.

My roommate was a bouncer at a strip club, Nikki VIP, so he helped me get a job there as a barback. During the days, I took more web design classes and picked up the occasional freelance design gig. At night, I kept the bar stocked and took out the trash at the strip club.

You might think working at a strip club was an exciting job for a young, heterosexual male. It was cool for about two weeks, then it became the most humiliating job I ever had. My friends would come in there to party, and here I am taking out the trash. Whenever someone would get too drunk and vomit in the club, I was the one who had to clean it up.

Plus, the club wasn't in the best part of town. One night, I was hauling garbage bags out of the back door when I heard gunshots from across the street. As I ducked back inside, I could hear the bullets whiz past, ricocheting off of the same metal dumpster into which I had just thrown some garbage bags.

I would come home around five a.m., my clothes reeking of beer, garbage, and cigarette smoke.

On slow nights at the club, I would be sitting behind the bar reading a textbook for one of my classes, totally unfazed by the naked girls surrounding me. I remember one night, one of the club's patrons randomly said to me, "You don't belong here. You stick out like a sore thumb." I found it odd that a complete stranger would say that to me, but I knew he was right.

When you're not aligned, the universe gives you signs.

I knew I needed to make a change, but I felt trapped. I needed the money.

Then a few weeks later, as I was getting dressed to go to work, the evening news was on the TV. The scene cut to breaking news of Club Nikki VIP being raided by the police. I couldn't believe my eyes! Helicopters hovered above the club where I worked. Police were taking all of the liquor out of the back door—the same liquor that I kept inventory of daily. I saw scantily clad strippers I knew being herded into the back of an Atlanta Police van.

The newscaster announced that Club Nikki had lost its liquor license. There were allegations of prostitution in the VIP rooms, scandals with the owner, and truthfully, the community didn't want the club around anymore.

That was it. The club was shut down. My job and my livelihood were gone in an instant. I didn't receive any severance pay, not even a phone call. That chapter was over. Another sign.

When you're not aligned, the universe gives you signs.

All hope wasn't lost, though. The club DJs and promoters had caught wind of my graphic design skills, so they hired me to design flyers and posters for their private parties and for other clubs. Hooray, now I was at least working *in my field*, something most college grads aspire to do, but I couldn't use any of this work in my portfolio. It was too raunchy.

Then one hot, humid night in June 2002, I was driving to meet one of the DJs at a different strip club, with the hopes of landing a new design gig. I needed the money badly. But I had never been to this club and didn't quite know where it was located (this was before turn-by-turn GPS directions were everywhere).

I got lost and kept trying to call the DJ to guide me to the club. But he was surrounded by loud music, so I couldn't hear him and he couldn't hear me. It was midnight, and I sat there at a stop sign, trying to get my bearings. I was the only car on the street. My windows were down because I couldn't afford to fix the air conditioner in my old Honda Civic. I had already lost my Cadillac because the head gasket blew, and I couldn't afford to get that fixed either.

Then seemingly out of nowhere, a man walked up to the side of my car and asked me for a ride. He looked homeless, and was wearing a mildew-smelling t-shirt and shorts. There's nothing strange about a homeless person approaching your vehicle on the streets of Atlanta, so I didn't feel alarmed. In fact, I asked him if he could help me find the club. He said that he knew where it was and agreed to show me if I gave him a ride. I really didn't want to let this guy in my car because he smelled so bad, but I thought of the story of the Good Samaritan from Sunday School, and I unlocked the passenger door for him.

Before I knew it, he pulled out a gun and pointed it at my chest. He yelled at me, "Get out of the car. You know what time it is! Leave the keys. Give me your phone and all of your money."

This was the first time I'd had a gun pointed at me at close range. I could feel the organs in my body retracting away from the nozzle as an involuntary fear response. When I looked into the robber's eyes, they were bloodshot red, and I could tell he was high on some type of drugs. I thought to myself, once he finds out I don't have any money, he is going to kill me.

So I gave him my phone and said, "Here, take my whole wallet," tossing it in his direction, knowing it was empty. That bought me enough time to take off running for my life. As I hopped over a wooden fence to safety, I heard the squeal of my car's tires screeching off into the distance behind me.

That was the scariest night of my life. Another sign.

When you're not aligned, the universe gives you signs.

That was the last sign I needed. That night, I metaphorically died and became someone else.

I thought of "The Parable of the Talents" (Matthew 25:14-30). I felt like God had blessed me with talents, and I was squandering them. At that point in my life, would God have said to me, "Well done, good and faithful servant"? No.

So I made a vow that night that I would never use my talents to promote anything distasteful ever again. And I have honored that vow ever since.

"So take the talent from him and give it to him who has the ten talents. For to everyone who has will more be given, and he will have an abundance. But from the one who has not, even what he has will be taken away."
—*Matthew 25: 28-29*

KEY TAKEAWAYS

- When you're not aligned with your true purpose, the universe gives you clues.
- You can either pay attention to those clues, or ignore them at your own peril.
- We each have talents. Once you discover your talents, seek wisdom for how you should use them in alignment with your purpose.

CHAPTER 4:
ALIGNMENT

"When life brings you full circle, pay attention. There's a lesson there."
—Mandy Hale

After the carjacking incident, I went through a tough wilderness period where I didn't have a car and I was depending on other people for rides. I was living in a one-bathroom apartment with four people, and I didn't have a job. Yet strangely, I felt happier and more at peace than ever before.

About a month later, I landed a full-time job as a graphic designer at a newspaper, eventually becoming the lead designer.

On my off time, I continued to serve freelance graphic and web design clients, but now I was landing much higher-profile clients like Tyler Perry, McDonald's, and some of the local radio stations.

Around the same time, that website that I launched in college—stuff-4GREEKS.com—started getting real orders from complete strangers around the country! Wow . . . I couldn't believe it. We were at the top of page one on Google for Greek paraphernalia-related keywords like "custom line jackets" (and we still are). This was before Google even offered sponsored ads, so we spent zero dollars on marketing back then.

My girlfriend, Monica, was in a sorority, so she and I decided to become business partners in stuff4GREEKS. We received a $300 order for some flyers, so we each put in another $350 of our own money and opened a business bank account with $1000.

This is the first version of stuff4GREEKS. We couldn't afford models, so I photoshopped Monica in the group photo 3 times.

The rest is history. We went from just designing the apparel to buying our own machines and actually making the jackets ourselves. Soon, I was able to leave my job and work in the business full-time. Monica left her job a year later, and we've never looked back.

Our first office was in Tyler Perry's building. Tyler and I worked out a deal for office space in exchange for discounted graphic design services. Working with Tyler was a big inspiration. He taught me to own my stuff and not be dependent on others.

We quickly outgrew that office and bought a bigger house so that we could buy more machines and move the business into our home basement.

After a few years, our business outgrew the house. We had two shifts of employees coming and going, and our neighbors started to complain about the cars. So we purchased an office building in West Midtown. The building was just a shell that had been sitting there empty. We built it from the ground up inside and relocated our offices there. Since we had some extra space and demand from our online customers, we opened a retail store there too.

We decided to call the retail store Zeus' Closet because we didn't want to limit ourselves to the fraternity and sorority market anymore.

Through many ups and downs, our business grew rapidly, and to our surprise, we were nominated for the Bulldog 100, an annual competition that recognizes the fastest-growing companies owned by UGA Alumni. At the time of this writing, we've made the list four times, but there was something very special about that first time. At the awards banquet, as we were each called up to the stage, would you believe who presented me with the award? It was UGA President Michael Adams, the very same president who had called me to his office and suspended me from college a decade earlier!

This was one of those defining moments.

I don't know if President Adams remembered me, but I sure remembered him.

It felt like I had come full circle, like I was now walking in alignment with God's purpose. I was finally on the right track.

I believe that in life, there are no coincidences. Everything happens for a reason.

When you are in alignment with your true purpose, the universe gives you clues. Pay attention to these clues, and pour double the energy into what's working.

At the time of this writing, Zeus' Closet has two brick-and-mortar locations, in addition to several e-commerce stores. That company generates well over six figures per month in revenue, and it is just one of the companies in our portfolio.

I'm now humbled to be able to share my story and teach entrepreneurs across the world. I've had the honor of sharing the stage with Gary

Vee, Grant Cardone, Arianna Huffington, and other legends.

Over the years, I have been privileged to travel the world for conferences, for speaking engagements, and just for fun. I even set a personal goal to visit every continent before age forty, and my goal was only foiled by inclement weather on the airport runway from the southern tip of South America to Antarctica. But hey, "Could be good, could be bad, who knows," right? I don't even like cold weather; I was just going to Antarctica to check the box.

I've been married to, and business partners with, that same girlfriend I started stuff4GREEKS with over twenty years ago—Monica—and we have two amazing kids, Imana and Legend.

I say none of this to brag but rather to point out that my *aligned* life is very different from my *misaligned* life. There is nothing more I want for you than to find alignment with your purpose because that will open so many doors for you. The next chapter will explain the mechanics for how you do that.

KEY TAKEAWAYS

- When you are not aligned with your true purpose, the universe will give you clues to help get you back on track. Pay attention.
- When you *are* aligned with your true purpose, the universe will also give you clues. You'll notice that synchronicities and quantum leaps start to happen in small areas of your life. Pay attention.
- The key is to recognize these clues and act accordingly. If you're out of alignment, change course. But when things are going well, double-down on what's working to capitalize on the momentum.

INSIGHTS

Use this space to write your reflections from this chapter.

What is one insight I learned about myself in regards to my alignment with my purpose?

_____

_____

_____

_____

_____

_____

_____

_____

_____

_____

_____

What is my commitment to action?

_____

_____

_____

_____

_____

_____

_____

_____

_____

_____

_____

CHAPTER 5:
SUBCONSCIOUS RESTRUCTURING

"Whatever we plant in our subconscious mind and nourish
with repetition and emotion will one day become a reality."
—*Earl Nightingale*

OVERVIEW

It was fall of 2016, and everything in my life felt cloudy and stagnant. I was an emotional mixed bag. At home, we were dealing with a two-year-old and a six-year-old, so there were fun moments, but the house was a mess and my mind felt messy and cluttered too. Business was steady, but we were strained by debt, so it felt like every dollar that came in the front door immediately went out the back door. We were in talks with acquiring another company, which on the surface seemed like a great opportunity, but something about it felt too good to be true.

To sum things up, I felt lost. I needed clarity. It felt like things were at a standstill. I was searching for answers and didn't know where to find them.

My friend Peter suggested that I try meditation. I had heard about meditation before, but it seemed woo-woo and boring to me. He insisted that I research Transcendental Meditation® (also known as "TM") and give it a try. My research revealed a roster of highly successful people that not only practice meditation, but also attribute much of their success to it—Jerry Seinfeld, Oprah, The Beatles, Russell Simmons, Tom Hanks, and Hugh Jackman—to name a few.[3]

At first I gave it a try on my own, but quickly became bored and frustrated. But I wanted the secrets that all of these famous people knew, so I paid around $1,000 USD to learn TM from a certified instructor. After four days of guided instruction followed by thirty consecutive days of meditation—twenty minutes in the morning and twenty minutes in the evening—I could feel the cobwebs start to clear in my brain.

I also bought a gratitude journal and would start and end each day by writing down three things for which I'm thankful. It felt like more goodness started coming my way.

I felt a renewed sense of clarity, like I was more in tune with the universe. I started making better decisions. We cleaned up the house. We implemented changes in our business model that made us more profitable and got us out of debt (more on this in later chapters). Things were unveiled to me about the business deal that I hadn't seen before, so we decided to pass on the opportunity. A month later, the company that we were in talks of acquiring went out of business. We had dodged a bullet.

One might say it is all just coincidence, but once I learned the science behind it, I credited my positive energy and clearer thinking to meditation and gratitude journaling. I then added the practice of written affirmations, which I will describe later.

---

[3] "Famous people who meditate, from A to Z," *Transcendental Meditation News & More*, August 10, 2017, https://tmhome.com/experiences/famous-people-who-meditate/

There are 4 purposes of subconscious restructuring:
1. Reduce stress and gain inner peace
2. Retrain your brain to notice positive reinforcements
3. Constant connection to the source of all answers
4. Alignment with the universe

The first thing we must understand is that all of our habits of thinking and acting are stored in the subconscious mind. Our subconscious mind has *memorized* all our comfort zones and works to keep us in them.

According to a study in *New Scientist* magazine, 95% of brain activity is unconscious. These include habits and patterns, automatic body function, creativity, emotions, personality, beliefs and values, cognitive biases, and long-term memory.

Moreover, this study goes on to share that up to 40% of behavior is habitual. And depending on the study you read, experts share that it takes anywhere from 15 days to over 250 days to form a new habit.

The subconscious mind powers the world.

The next thing we must accept is that there's more invisible stuff than there is visible matter. Your subconscious brain communicates via invisible signals. Has someone ever yawned near you, then you immediately started yawning too? Those are mirror neurons firing in the brain.

Think about radio frequencies. Cell signals. Satellite signals. Wi-fi. FaceTime. Zoom. All of these things communicate over frequencies that you cannot see. But just because you cannot see them doesn't mean they are not powerful. In fact, the opposite is true.

Tony Robbins says business is a spiritual game. Some people are scared off by the word "spirituality," but really, prayer, meditation, and stillness are all a means of doing the same things: quieting the mind, restructuring the subconscious, and tapping into a higher source for answers.

Spirituality is actually scientific.

With that said, *how* do we reprogram our subconscious?

WORDS CREATE REALITY

Thoughts are things. The moment you have a thought, neurons are firing in your brain, and that thought now exists in the universe.

Then when you speak that thought, the energy changes form into sound waves and causes vibrations that impact the world on levels we can't yet see.

The vibrations cause someone to take action (maybe you, maybe someone else), a chain of events is set in motion, and the words eventually become an actual thing.

This is how inventions are born.

This is why, when you have an idea and don't act on it, someone else will. The idea already exists, and it will eventually manifest itself in the physical space.

Albert Einstein is often credited with saying that "Energy cannot be created or destroyed; it can only be changed from one form to another." That is what happens with your thoughts and ideas; they just change form.

Thoughts become words.
Words become actions.
Actions become habits.

Habits become reputation.
Reputation becomes character.
Character becomes destiny.

With that said, it is very important to guard your thoughts (the words you speak silently to yourself) and the words you speak out loud because they shape your entire world.

Try replacing the following words and phrases in your vocabulary:

Loser language	Winner words
"can't"	"Let's figure out how"
"try"	"do" or "do not"
"hope"	"plan"
"if"	"when"
"problem"	"challenge"
"why"	"what" or "how"
"but"	"and"
"I don't know"	"Let's find out"

We actually have a sign in our company restroom reminding all team members that these words are not allowed. They just don't fit with our company values and culture.

The word "can't" reinforces a defeatist attitude, a victim mentality. If someone else can do it, so can you. You just need to be resourceful and figure out how.

Another noncommittal, wimpy word is "try." Like Yoda says, "Do or do not. There is no try." Ever ask someone to do something and they said, "I'll try"? Chances are it won't happen. They've already given themselves an out.

Instead of "hope," we plan. There's no action from hope.

And instead of the word "if," we say "when." Try incorporating this into your sales conversations. For example, "*When* you place your order . . ."

Instead of "problems" we have "challenges" because problems can seem insurmountable, but we look forward to overcoming challenges.

Instead of "why," we reframe the question using "what" or "how" because the word "why" can sound accusatory. For example, if I ask you "Why are you late?" you may be taken aback. But if I ask, "What can we change to help you arrive earlier next time?" it sounds more solution-oriented and less abrasive.

Instead of "but," we say "and" because the word "but" negates everything that you said before it in that sentence. For example, "I want to help you move, but I have to wash my hair."

Instead of "I don't know," we say, "Let's find out." In these modern times, we have infinite knowledge at our fingertips. When someone says, "I don't know," he is simply dismissing responsibility. You can always find out the answer or use deductive logic to figure out where the answer might be.

ASSESSMENT

To improve our "S" area—**Subconscious Restructuring, Spirituality, Stillness, the Self**—let's start with an honest assessment. Grade yourself on a scale of 1–10, but remember this: you are grading yourself for this particular moment in time—how you're feeling today, right now. You are not criticizing yourself and saying, "This is just how I am."

Don't judge your score. There is no good or bad. Replace self-judgment with curiosity. And be honest. Don't grade yourself aspirationally.

Here are some examples. For your "S" area, a score of 1 might mean: You feel brain fog. No clarity. Things just seem to be "off" right now. You feel like you're being reactive instead of being proactive . . . like your day, your schedule, and your thoughts are all being pushed around by external forces. Because of this, you probably feel a sense of confusion, frustration, and sadness. As high performers, we're often faced with high levels of stress and anxiety. This can lead to lack of focus, high blood pressure, memory loss, impaired sleep, and more.

In contrast, a score of 10 for your "S" area would mean you're in a state of flow. The right thoughts and ideas just come to you. Every word that you say lands perfectly. Your timing for every action is impeccable. You feel like you are accessing your brain's full capabilities—like Bradley Cooper's character in the movie *Limitless*, or Scarlett Johansson's character in the movie *Lucy*. We've all had days or moments where we've felt this way. That would be a perfect 10.

So where do you fall on a scale of 1–10? Use space in the companion journal to record your "S" score for today, along with any accompanying thoughts or reflections around your score. To get your companion journal, visit **www.simplesuccess.school**.

EXERCISES

So what do you do if you are currently feeling deficient in your "S" area? Start each day with this three-step process:

GRATITUDE

Start every single day by grabbing a pen and writing down three things you are thankful for.

Based on research from The HeartMath Institute, EKG charts show that when a person shifts from frustration to appreciation, their heart activity and brain waves become aligned.[4]

Use the companion journal to guide you through this exercise. If you need a journal, visit **www.simplesuccess.school**.

AFFIRMATIONS

Next, think of one goal that you wish to bring into reality. Craft that goal into a concise sentence and write it fifteen times. Very important: just write the goal, not the how. When you give your subconscious mind a strong "what" and a strong "why," it will figure out the "how" in due course.

This exercise is very much like the gratitude exercise in Step 1; you are just expressing thanks in advance.

World-famous cartoonist Scott Adams, creator of Dilbert, attributes his success in large part to written affirmations. He reportedly wrote the

---

[4] Rollin McCraty, Ph.D., "The Science of HeartMath," https://www.heartmath.com/science/

sentence "I, Scott Adams, will become a syndicated cartoonist" fifteen times a day, and it became true.

Adams says, "The idea behind affirmations is that you simply write down your goals fifteen times a day and somehow, as if by magic, coincidences start to build until you achieve your objective against all odds."

Magic is just science that we haven't figured out yet.

If you were to travel 500 years in the past and somehow show someone a working airplane or a working iPhone, they would probably accuse you of dark magic and burn you at the stake.

MEDITATION

The third exercise is meditation. There are nine different types of meditation, and here is a quick overview of each:

Breath Awareness Meditation – great for starters and getting into the process

Metta Meditation – loving and kindness to ourselves and others

Body Scan Meditation – moving from the bottom of your body to the top, concentrate on certain areas of the body at a time

Progressive Relaxation Meditation – this helps the entire body and mind to relax at the same time

Thought Observation (Zen) Meditation – pick a specific thought and observe it as it moves through your mind, and see where it goes

Truth-Seeking Meditation – using high-intonation breathing to open your mind to a higher source for answers

Incantation Meditation – repeating a phrase that we really want to instill within ourselves

Transformational Meditation – a way to transform our beliefs, values, emotions, or behaviors

Transcendental Meditation® – repeating a meaningless word, to declutter the mind and tap into deeper levels of consciousness

One form of meditation is not necessarily better than another; you must choose the meditation practice that is best for you and the purpose you are trying to achieve.

As mentioned earlier, I personally practice Transcendental Meditation® ("TM"). TM is a mantra-based meditation. Famous comedian Jerry Seinfeld says that "Transcendental Meditation is like having a charger for your whole body and mind." He has been practicing this daily ritual for over forty years, and he says it "will help you to take things more easy."[5]

I will give you very basic instructions for TM here, but I suggest going to https://www.tm.org/ to find a certified practitioner and get the full experience:

Pick a mantra that feels comfortable. A mantra is a meaningless word. You can refer to the list below for some suggested mantras by age.

---

[5] "Jerry Seinfeld: "Transcendental Meditation is a charger for your body and mind," *Transcendental Meditation News & More*, February 17, 2016, https://tmhome.com/experiences/jerry-seinfeld-video-on-transcendental-meditation-a-charger-for-your-body-and-mind/

Popular mantras by age

AGE	MANTRA
0-11	eng
12-13	em
14-15	enga
16-17	ema
18-19	ieng
20-21	iem
22-23	ienga
24-25	iema
26-29	shirim
30-34	shiring
35-39	kirim
40-44	kiring
45-49	hirim
50-54	hiring
55-59	sham
60	shama

Sit on a chair in a quiet place with your feet flat on the floor, your back straight, and your head erect. Place your hands comfortably in your lap. Close your eyes and repeat your mantra in your mind only, while breathing in and out in a calm and regular rhythm. Concentrate on maintaining your posture and breathing. Concentrate on repeating your mantra. If you become aware that your mind has wandered, just bring it back to your mantra. Don't judge it.

If you fall asleep, that's okay. Again, do not judge your meditation practice.

Do this for twenty minutes, twice per day.

Again, this is not meant to be a substitute for the full training.

At the beginning and end of each day, take time to restructure your subconscious through gratitude journaling, written affirmations, and meditation. These practices are scientifically proven to reduce anxiety, lower blood pressure, and improve mental clarity.

Your action item is to complete the Gratitude, Affirmations, and Meditation sections in the journal, first thing in the morning and last thing at night for the next thirty days. We've also included a calendar so that you can tape it to your bathroom mirror and keep a consistent winning streak.

For in-depth access to our guided Gratitude, Affirmation, and Meditation courses, visit **www.simplesuccess.school.**

SUPPLEMENTS

There are supplements called nootropics that supposedly boost brain power and clarity. I personally have not had success with any of them, so I cannot recommend them at this time.

The way I test supplements is to try them for thirty days. After that, I will assess whether the net results are positive, neutral, or negative (due to side effects) for me. If they are neutral or negative, I stop using the supplement.

Search the word "nootropics" to discover an entire world of legal smart drugs. In my experience, they are expensive and ineffective, but your experience may be different.

Some over-the-counter mind supplements that I have personally tried and found to be beneficial are:

5-HTP – 5-HTP increases the production of serotonin in the brain and central nervous system. Serotonin can affect sleep, appetite, temperature, sexual behavior, and pain sensation. Some studies indicate that 5-HTP may improve symptoms of depression in some people and might even work as well as some prescription antidepressant drugs.[6]

GABA – GABA blocks certain brain signals and decreases activity in your nervous system, which keeps you calm. This enables the body and mind to relax and fall asleep. One small study of thirteen adults showed GABA to be effective as a relaxant and anxiety reliever, and some evidence even suggests that GABA may help reduce high blood pressure.[7]

Tobacco-free nicotine mints – It is widely known that nicotine in tobacco brings illness and death to millions of people. However, according to research, the regular use of nicotine in **its purest form** (meaning *without* smoking or tobacco) may potentially enhance cognitive performance, and protect against Parkinson's disease, Tourette's disease, and Alzheimer's disease.[8]

KEY TAKEAWAYS

- Starting the day with gratitude is proven to reduce stress that stems from comparison to someone else, or to an ideal version of yourself.
- Handwritten affirmations can be stronger than verbal affirmations because they reinforce the thoughts in our physical muscles and involves multiple senses.
- Meditation is like sweeping away the cobwebs in the attic of our

---

[6] WedMD, *5-Htp – Uses, Side Effects, And More,* https://www.webmd.com/vitamins/ai/ingredientmono-794/5-htp

[7] Michael J. Breus Ph.D., "3 Amazing Benefits of GABA," *Psychology Today,* January 3, 2019, https://www.psychologytoday.com/us/blog/sleep-newzzz/201901/3-amazing-benefits-gaba

[8] Dan Hurley, "Will a Nicotine Patch Make You Smarter? [Excerpt]," *Scientific American,* February 9, 2014, https://www.scientificamerican.com/article/will-a-nicotine-patch-make-you-smarter-excerpt/

brain and organizing our thoughts to allow for higher-level thinking that transcends the normal realm of consciousness. Countless high-performing athletes and celebrities attribute their success to a consistent meditation practice.

INSIGHTS

Use this space to write your reflections from this chapter.

What is one insight I learned about myself in regards to my spiritual practice?

_____

_____

_____

_____

_____

_____

_____

_____

_____

_____

What is my commitment to action?

_____

_____

_____

_____

_____

_____

_____

_____

_____

_____

CHAPTER 6:
INTELLECTUAL IMPROVEMENT &
IMPLEMENTATION

"Intellectual growth should commence at birth, and cease only at death."
—Albert Einstein

"Be like a sponge, and soak up knowledge."
—Dr. Joanne Williams (my mom ☺)

OVERVIEW

In my early twenties, I worked at the *Thrifty Nickel*, a classifieds newspaper. After a long stint of unstable income from freelance gigs, I was happy to land a job there as a graphic designer.

The job paid $14 per hour, and it was a long drive across town, but the schedule was perfect for my lifestyle at the time. I worked twelve hours per day, three days per week (only Monday through Wednesday) because it was a weekly paper, and I had to get the files to the printer every Wednesday night to meet the deadline. The rest of the week I had off, to focus on my freelance clients and my side businesses.

On Mondays and Tuesdays at the *Thrifty Nickel*, we got a chance to flex our creative muscles a little, designing ads for car dealerships, estate sales, real estate agents, and internal promotions. The latter half of Tuesday and all day Wednesday we spent paginating the paper, which means laying everything out and making sure the spacing between letters and lines was all correct. Basically, it was the boring part of graphic design work. At this point in the process, it didn't require reading any words or coming up with anything creative; it was more like solving a puzzle or playing a game of Tetris for hours and hours. So naturally, I donned my headphones and listened to music while I plowed through each section of the paper.

I would typically listen to rap music—whatever the latest album was—over and over on repeat. But then I grew tired of the music and discovered Internet radio. I liked listening to Clark Howard and learning the latest ways to save money. Then something made me explore business talk radio (this was the predecessor to podcasts).

One night, I stumbled upon an interview with an author named Vincent Roazzi, who had recently published a book called *The Spirituality of Success: Getting Rich with Integrity*. The interview caught my attention because, growing up in the church, I was taught that wanting to be rich was a bad thing and would damn me to hell.

In fact, this particular Bible passage was buried deep in my subconscious:

> *Jesus answered, "If you want to be perfect, go, sell your possessions and give to the poor, and you will have treasure in heaven. Then come, follow me. When the young man heard this, he went away sad, because he had great wealth.*

> *Then Jesus said to his disciples, "Truly I tell you, it is hard for someone who is rich to enter the kingdom of heaven. Again I tell you, it is easier for a camel to go through the eye of a needle than for someone who is rich to enter the kingdom of God."*
> *—Matthew 19: 21-24*

I wanted to be rich. I loved watching the TV show *Lifestyles of the Rich and Famous* as a kid. But my family attended a very traditional church every Sunday, so you can imagine the conflicting feelings and the guilt associated with my secret desires.

The interview with Vincent Roazzi was the first time I had ever heard the words "getting rich" combined with "spirituality" and "integrity" in a positive way. I was instantly intrigued, so I immediately purchased the book and devoured it.

That book changed my life and sent me down a rabbit hole of reading more personal development and business books. I followed Jim Rohn, Tony Robbins, Robert Kiyosaki, Napoleon Hill, Deepak Chopra, and countless others, trying to get my hands on everything published or recorded by some of these famous authors. Then I discovered audiobooks and spent every minute while driving or working at the newspaper, consuming their content.

I never came out of that rabbit hole. In fact, I've only dug deeper for the past twenty years, listening to books and podcasts nonstop, researching, reading articles, attending seminars and conferences, joining organizations, taking courses, and investing hundreds of thousands of dollars in mastermind groups and coaching programs.

Jim Rohn famously said, "You are the average of the five people you spend the most time with." This doesn't just mean your friends and family members. Through various media, I spend time with some of the world's greatest thinkers, inventors, multimillionaires and billionaires, living and dead. This has changed the way that I fundamentally think and is now reflected in my investment accounts and lifestyle.

Your quest to absorb knowledge must be constant and never-ending.

ASSESSMENT

You're reading this book, so I assume you have a thirst for learning, but let's take a full, honest assessment of your "I" area—**Intellectual Improvement and Implementation.**

Grade yourself on a scale of 1–10, and remember: You are grading yourself for this particular moment in time—how you're feeling today, right now. Don't judge your responses. There is no good or bad. Replace self-judgment with curiosity. And be honest. Don't grade yourself aspirationally.

For your "I" area, a score of 1 might mean you feel like you're the dumbest person in every room lately. You aren't learning anything new, your brain isn't being challenged, and you feel stagnant. You know this is a problem because somewhere out there, two kids in a garage are building the next thing that will disrupt your business and/or industry.

In contrast, a score of 10 for your "I" area might mean: You digest new information daily. You have all of the Blinkist app badges. You're on Audible's Premium Plus plan, and you still run out of credits halfway through the year. You feel smart. You're constantly attending conferences, workshops, and learning events. You're constantly innovating in your company. People come to you to learn new things.

So where do you fall on a scale of 1–10? Use space in the companion journal to record your "I" score for today, along with any accompanying thoughts or reflections around your score.

EXERCISES

If you're feeling deficient in the area of Intellectual Improvement, here's what to do:

INCREASE THE <u>AMOUNT</u> OF QUALITY INPUT

Supposedly, in the early days of Warren Buffett's career, he would read 600–1,000 pages in a single day. Nowadays, he still dedicates 80% of his day to reading.

How to increase the amount of learning content you consume:

Listen to audiobooks at a fast speed while exercising and driving.

Try speed reading. Here are some pointers: use an object, like a pen, to move along the lines of the text. As your eyes follow quickly, your subconscious will catch the gist of the information. You can also try reading the first and last sentence of each paragraph.

Try Blinkist for audio book summaries.

Attend learning events.

WHEN YOU ENCOUNTER EXTREMELY USEFUL, RELEVANT INFORMATION, GO DEEPER

Buy the print version of the book and read it while you listen to the audiobook too.

Remember that audio learning, visual learning, experiential learning, and reading written words are all different. Each one works a different area of the brain. Consume important information in as many different ways as possible.

To make learning stick, write it down, teach it, share it on social media.

Hire a coach or trainer on the subject.

Join a mastermind or accountability group.

CAPTURE IDEAS QUICKLY, BEFORE THEY GET AWAY

As you increase your rate of learning from different sources, cross-pollination of ideas will start to happen. These are the ideas that, if implemented, can lead to innovative breakthroughs in your business and life.

Here are some ways to capture ideas:

Write in a dream journal as soon as you wake up.

When on the go, use voice dictation to store notes on your phone or in your reminders or in a Google Doc.

With the Braintoss app, you can quickly email a note to yourself using your voice.

When in the shower, use Aqua Notes, a waterproof notepad and pencil that stick to your shower wall.

You want to capture ideas quickly so that you can apply them at the right time. Don't think to yourself, "Oh, I'll remember it later." You won't. Capture it now.

INNOVATION = INFORMATION + IDEAS + IMPLEMENTATION

I remember one time we were on a family vacation at the beach. As we walked along the boardwalk, I noticed a kiosk that was printing custom license plates and cell phone covers on the spot.

At the time, in our business, we were selling custom license plates, but we outsourced them to another company, and that company had become unreliable with fulfilling orders on time. I figured, if this lady in this kiosk has figured out how to print her hard goods on demand, then surely we can do it too.

So I took a mental inventory of the model numbers of her equipment. We ultimately bought our own equipment, fired our vendor, and brought the license plate manufacturing in-house. This increased our revenue by 10% and also improved our margins on that product line by 82%.

This is an example of innovation happening due to the combination of information (the equipment model numbers), plus ideas (the idea of printing custom tourist gifts, combined with our need for a reliable vendor), plus implementation. Nothing happens unless you take action.

EXERCISES

For the next thirty days, read at least twenty pages in a book on a new subject, or listen to twenty minutes of an audiobook. That is the first step to improving your learning score.

KEY TAKEAWAYS

- First, increase the amount of knowledge you consume.
- Then go deeper in specific, relevant areas.
- Capture ideas fast, before they leave your mind.
- Combine ideas and concepts that you've learned.
- Take action.

INSIGHTS

Use this space to write your reflections from this chapter.

What is one insight I learned about myself in regards to my intellectual journey?

_____

_____

_____

_____

_____

_____

_____

_____

_____

_____

What is my commitment to action?

_____

_____

_____

_____

_____

_____

_____

_____

_____

_____

CHAPTER 7:
MONEY MASTERY

"Cash is the oxygen of independence."
—Morgan Housel, Psychology of Money

OVERVIEW

I didn't go to business school, and growing up in my household, we didn't talk about money. So I spent a lot of my life mishandling money and learning financial lessons the hard way.

As a young adult, I remember being so broke that some nights I'd only have pasta noodles with ketchup for dinner. Now I'm able to treat my family to the finest restaurants, without even flinching when the waiter brings the check.

I remember having over $500,000 in credit card debt and feeling trapped in a vicious cycle of interest, late fees, and minimum payments. Now, I'm completely debt free, aside from the house I live in and one small business loan.

Money used to seem like a foreign language to me, but I learned it, and so can you. In this chapter, I will break it down in a way so simple that anyone can understand it and get rich.

Think about money the same way you think about oxygen. Not having enough oxygen is dangerous and feels life-threatening. Having excess amounts of oxygen doesn't add that much to your quality of life, but the knowledge that it is abundant and unlimited in supply gives you peace of mind. You feel better knowing there is unlimited oxygen, and you can breathe as deeply as you like, as often as you like, without worry. You can sleep soundly. You can do things you want without stress or strain because there is more than enough oxygen for everyone.

Money is the same way. There is more than enough money for everyone, and it is all around us. Visualize the millions of digital transactions happening every second, passing through the air and through your body right now. Now open your heart and your mind to receive more of that which flows through you. This is the mindset I want you to have as you digest this chapter.

Warning: Some of the money-handling techniques that I'm going to teach you will seem strange because they're not how most people handle money. But do you really want to model yourself after most people? Most people are broke, and I don't want you to be one of them, so do the opposite of what most people do.

WHAT IS TRUE FINANCIAL WEALTH?

I used to think that once you become a millionaire, you've made it, all of your money woes are gone forever, and you live happily ever after. I couldn't have been more wrong. I know multimillionaires who are depressed and on the brink of bankruptcy.

So what is true wealth, then?

In simplest terms, wealth is the ratio of your means to your wants and needs.

For example, if Heather brings home $10,000 per month, and her living expenses are only $5,000 every month, then Heather is wealthy because her ratio of income to expenses is 2 to 1.

In contrast, meet Sam. Let's say Sam brings home $100,000 per month, but his living expenses are $120,000 per month. This means Sam is really poor because he is operating at a deficit.

Since Sam makes more money than Heather, on the surface it looks like he is wealthier than she is. But actually, Heather is the wealthier of the two. Heather also probably sleeps better than Sam because he is likely racking up debt and interest to cover the additional $240,000 per year that it costs him to maintain his lifestyle after using up his earned income. With the added financial stress, Sam is likely stressed out, overweight, and looks older than his biological age. More on the physical impacts of stress in the next chapter.

The purpose of this example is to illustrate that **wealth is not defined by a dollar amount**. Neither a high salary nor a high-revenue business nor having millions in a bank account are true indicators of wealth.

Instead, wealth is a **ratio** of income to expenses.

To determine your *wealth score*, take your total monthly income, and divide that number by your total monthly expenses. The higher the number the better.

Write your totals below. Be sure to include everything in your total—rent/mortgage, car note, insurance, gas, utilities, food, entertainment, clothes, travel, etc.

Income $_____

divided by

Expenses $_____

= _____

In our story above, Happy Heather's wealth ratio is $10,000 income to $5,000 expenses. So Heather's score is 2.

Income $10,000

divided by

Expenses $5,000

= 2

Stressed-out Sam, on the other hand, has a wealth ratio of $100,000 income to $120,000 expenses. So Sam's score is 0.83.

Income $100,000

divided by

Expenses $120,000

= 0.83

Health check: Ideally, you want your wealth score always to be 1.5 or higher. If your score is lower than 1, then we have some work to do.

Let me make one thing clear: I am not advocating that you live below your means as many financial gurus will advise. I've never heard of anyone who became financially independent just by skipping lattes. Instead, my approach is to cut out every expense that you are only lukewarm about (remember Principle 1), and to *expand your means* so that you can live the lifestyle you desire.

How can you expand your means? Keep reading for some action steps.

ASSESSMENT

Money has an emotional component. Let's say you have a healthy wealth score of 2 from the exercise above, but you're depressed because you really want it to be 4. If the gap between your current reality and your ideal reality emotionally bothers you, then your *overall* "M" (Money Mastery) score would still be low.

Let's assess your overall "M" score, factoring in your current emotions around **Money Mastery**. Grade yourself on a scale of 1–10, and remember, you are grading yourself for this particular moment in time—how you're feeling today, right now. And be honest. Don't grade yourself aspirationally.

One thing, though. Regardless of your emotions, if your wealth score from above is less than 1, then that means you definitely have a low "M" score overall because being financially upside down is not healthy.

Some signs of a low "M" score might be: your accounts are in the negative, you're buried in debt, and money problems keep you up at night. If you're a business owner with a low "M" score, the business is losing money, and you struggle to meet payroll. Life and business can be tough if you're operating on razor-thin margins.

In contrast, an "M" score of perfect 10 would be: you're debt free, and you have enough money to do what you want, wherever you want, with whoever you want, for as long as you want. This is ultimate financial freedom.

So where do you fall on a scale of 1–10? Use space in the companion journal to record your "M" score for today, along with any accompanying thoughts or reflections around your score.

Now it's time for some action. If you're feeling deficient in the area of Money Mastery, here are some action tips for you that I've categorized into two areas:

Growing a profitable business

Personal money management

GROWING A PROFITABLE BUSINESS

Even if you are an employee working a nine-to-five job, do NOT skip this section. It still applies to you because I believe that everyone should own a business—even if it is just a side business, at a minimum—so that you can take advantage of the tax benefits and gain more control over your financial future. Owning a profitable business is your vehicle for *expanding your means.*

The progression of your business journey might look something like the sequence below, but you could stop at any phase, or skip a phase, or even be involved with multiple businesses in different roles:

- Employee
- Employee with a side hustle
- Fully self-employed "solopreneur"
- Small business owner with a few employees
- Mid-size business owner
- Chairperson of an enterprise
- Investor with advisory role
- Majority shareholder of a public company
- Passive investor

As you work your way through these phases, the goal is to ultimately have all of your income generated by investments that require very little active input from you. This is called *passive income.* The end game is for your money to work for you, generating passive income through assets you own.

A few examples of passive income are:
- Selling digital information products
- Rental income
- Peer-to-peer lending
- Stocks and bonds
- Create an app
- REITs – real estate investment trusts
- Rent out your home short-term
- Advertise on your car

You have achieved true financial independence when your passive income exceeds your living expenses.

My friend and mentee, Juan Pablo, founder of 100 Percent Financed, came up with an easy way to remember this; he calls it "The PILE Formula":

PASSIVE INCOME > LIVING EXPENSES

This mindset was inspired by Robert Kiyosaki's classic book *Rich Dad, Poor Dad.*

But we are getting ahead of ourselves. Let's start with where you are and move through each step.

START: FROM EMPLOYEE TO SELF-EMPLOYED

If you're an employee, start a side hustle during your off hours. That's how we grew stuff4GREEKS in its infancy; my wife and I were both employees with full-time jobs, and we spent our evenings and days off working on our side business.

Wondering what type of business to start? First ask yourself these questions:

What are some of my hobbies?

What do other people say I'm good at?

What skills or talents do I have that other people ask me questions about?

For example, if you're into fitness, you could be an online trainer as a side job. If you're into relationships, you could be a dating coach. Love to travel? You could be a travel blogger and/or YouTuber on the side.

> Additional resources: If you need more help with starting your side hustle, check out the *Become Your Own Boss* program at **www.simplesuccess.school**.

You can accomplish so much with just two to three hours of daily effort focused on your side hustle. And on the weekends, you can devote a lot more time to growing your business.

Here's an example schedule that might work if you have a typical nine-to-five job with an hour commute each way:

6:00 a.m. Wake up, exercise while listening to business audiobooks and/or podcasts

Later in this book, we will discuss the full morning routine for manifesting massive success in your life.

7:00 a.m. Shower, get dressed

8:00 a.m. Commute to work while listening to business audiobooks and/or podcasts

9:00 a.m. – 5:00 p.m. Work at your job

Mindset tip: Don't think of yourself as an employee. You are the CEO of Your Name, LLC, and your employer is your biggest client. Your goal is to OVER-deliver world-class service to your client so that they can't imagine doing business without you.

5:00 p.m. – 6:00 p.m. Commute home while listening to business audiobooks and/or podcasts

6:00 p.m. – 8:00 p.m. Dinner, family time, recreation

8:00 p.m. – 10:30 p.m. Work on your side business

10:30 p.m. – 11:00 p.m. Wind down, night routine

11:00 p.m. – 6:00 a.m. Sleep

Of course, you could sleep less, but sleep is vital for your cognitive awareness and overall health. The average person needs six to eight hours of sleep every night. I do not advocate sacrificing your sleep long term, but I'd be doing you a disservice if I didn't confess that I've pulled many all-nighters whenever I was deep in the throes of a project and didn't want to break the momentum. Heck, I've pulled some all-nighters to finish this book. But I also strategically make time to allow for deep recovery through a combination of power naps and weekend sleep catch-up. More on the importance of sleep in the chapter on Physical Presence.

With the above schedule, you are devoting 12.5 hours during the week to your side hustle. Find another 12.5 hours on the weekend, and you are devoting 25 hours per week to your side hustle. That's 100 hours per month. With 100 hours of intentional execution on your side business, you will soon get to the point where you are making the same amount of money in your side business as you are in your day job. This is a wonderful feeling!

How to create more time in your day:

If you're thinking "but I don't have time to start a side business," then refer back to *Guiding Principle #1: Eliminate the lukewarm.*

Cut out one or more of these things below that you might be just lukewarm about:

TV series—Search for the recaps on YouTube.

Sports games—If you feel like you must catch the game real-time, have it muted in the background while you work, and/or only watch the highlights later. The commercials and commentary are a waste of time.

Happy hours/socializing—Save these moments as a reward to yourself for when you accomplish a milestone in your business.

Notifications—Keep your phone on Do Not Disturb or Focus mode. I turn off *all* notifications in my phone settings, except for phone calls and text messages. I also turn off all sounds, dings, pop-ups, and notifications on my computer. Studies show that for every interruption, it takes an average of 23 minutes 15 seconds to get back on track.[9]

Things you should *not* be lukewarm about: learning, growing, expressing gratitude, exercising, eating right, drinking water, and nurturing positive relationships. These are things that you do *not* want to eliminate in effort to save time because integrating them into your life ultimately *adds* time to your days.

---

[9] Kristin Wong, "How Long It Takes to Get Back on Track After a Distraction," *Lifehacker*, July 29, 2015, https://lifehacker.com/how-long-it-takes-to-get-back-on-track-after-a-distract-1720708353

Aside from the extra income, another benefit of owning your own business is that you can write off a lot of expenditures on your taxes, even if your business isn't making money yet. As long as the expense is incurred with the *intent* of leading to a sale, it is likely tax deductible. That means if you treat a prospect to dinner, or host a company party, or take clients to a ball game, all or some of the expense could be tax-deductible, as long as you keep good records documenting the business intent, should you ever be audited. You could also possibly write off a portion of your personal rent and utilities if you have a home office. You could also possibly write off some business-related vehicle expenses.

Note: I am not a tax attorney, and this is not tax advice. Please check with your tax attorney or CPA about your specific situation and what may or may not be deductible for you. Also, laws change every year.

At some point, you'll start earning enough money from your side hustle to make it your main hustle and quit your full-time job. You'll know when you reach this point because you'll do the math and start thinking to yourself, "How much would my business grow if I devoted an additional forty hours per week to it, instead of devoting those forty hours to my current employer?"

I will never forget the day I realized that I could replace my job income working fully on my own. I still have a copy of my resignation letter in my file cabinet. My manager asked me, "What are you going to do now?" She knew about my side business but had no idea how much it had grown. I think she feared that I had found a better job or that I was going to work for a competitor. Something came over me, and I replied with a sense of knowing, "I am going to work in my own business full time, and I'm never going to work for anyone else ever again. I don't mean that in an arrogant way, I just know that I've been called to do this." It's almost as if the words came from a different place, or from a higher power, but I heard my voice saying them.

I meant it with 100% of my being. That day—April 10, 2004—was my last day being an employee.

SCALE: FROM SELF-EMPLOYED TO BUSINESS OWNER

Whether you have one foot or both feet in the self-employed phase, congratulations . . . you are now your own boss. You own your own job! There is a sense of freedom that comes with this, but also a lot of hard work because it's all on you.

There is an old joke/saying that is usually some variation of this: "Being my own boss is great because I get to choose my own schedule! I get to choose *which* sixteen hours I work every day!"

To get out of this cycle and move from self-employed to small business owner, you'll need to hire staff and implement systems so they can do the work for you.

Additional resources: For more help with growing your business, visit **www.simplesuccess.school** and check out the programs *Roadmap To Your First Million* and *How To Run a $1M/Year Business.*

SYSTEMATIZE: OWNING A BUSINESS THAT WORKS FOR YOU

Making the jump from being a "solopreneur" to being a true business owner first requires implementing systems in your business. Here's how to develop Standard Operating Procedures (SOPs):

Start by keeping a time log of everything you do in a day. Then we are going to E.A.T. each task.

First, look at each task and ask yourself, "Do we really *need* to do this? What would happen if we didn't?" If you can live without it, Eliminate it (E).

Then look at each task and see if there is a way to Automate it (A).

Services like Zapier and IFTTT help with task automation.

Perhaps your phone line can be semi-automated with informational recordings; we use *Onebox* for this.

Marketing emails can be automated with Mailchimp, Keap, or Active Campaign, among others.

Use TextExpander to create shortcuts for long messages that you type over and over.

Those are just a few examples. With research, you'll find that a lot of repetitive tasks can be automated with software.

If you can't Eliminate it (E) or Automate it (A), then Train (T) someone else to do it. Start with the tasks that are most straightforward and repetitive, and type up the step-by-step instructions to complete those tasks.

If you have a task that can be handled remotely, great. Type up the description and list it on Fiverr or Upwork. Make sure you agree on a flat rate to complete each task, not an hourly rate.

Try out different providers until you have a reliable person to execute that task on a regular basis. It should be easy to try different providers for these tasks because all you have to do is copy/paste the step-by-step instructions.

For positions where you need to have someone come in and work in person, try a similar approach, but you will likely give that person more than one task to complete each day.

Soon you will end up with an instruction manual full of step-by-step documents for each task. Each time a new person comes on board, go through the documents and teach them the steps, then have them update anything that has changed.

Use supplemental photos, checklists, diagrams, and instructional videos to enhance the learning materials over time.

You can keep everything organized in Google Docs or Word Docs with folders at first. Then when you outgrow that and want to implement testing capabilities, and track completion of certain modules, consider a user-based learning management system like Trainual or Membervault.

Books every business owner must read about implementing systems:

- *The E-Myth Revisited,* by Michael Gerber
- *Work The System,* by Sam Carpenter
- *2-Second Lean,* by Paul Akers
- *The Checklist Manifesto,* by Atul Gawande

Once everything in your business is either automated or handled by someone else, and your day-to-day is freed up to work on the business, not in it, then you own a machine that works for you. Congratulations, you are no longer just self-employed. You are now a business owner.

THE RULE OF 26

There are three key numbers that drive your business:
- Number of new clients
- Average order value (AOV)
- Repeat purchase frequency

If you increase each one of these numbers by just 26%, then you will double your revenue.

For example, if you have 100 clients, an AOV of $10,000, and your average repeat purchase frequency is 2, then you currently have $2M in revenue. Increase each one of these numbers by 26%, and you will have $4M in revenue.

I call this The Rule of 26.

	# of clients	AOV	repeat purchase frequency	revenue
current	100	$10,000.00	2	$2,000,000.00
increase by	26%	26%	26%	
result	126	$12,600.00	2.52	$4,000,752.00

200.04% total growth

Additional resources: To access the above spreadsheet and plug in your own numbers, visit **www.simplesuccess.school** and click on *The Double Your Revenue Dashboard.*

HOW TO GET MORE LEADS

Here are some ways to increase your number of leads, because the more leads you have, the more you can convert into clients:

- Ask your existing clients for referrals
- Over-deliver "raving fan," impeccable service to your existing clients
- Social media marketing
- Referrals, word of mouth
- Content marketing—blog, YouTube, newsjacking
- Start a podcast
- Be a guest on podcasts
- Trade shows
- Case studies
- Buy leads
- Cold calling
- Networking events
- Surveys
- Billboards
- Press releases
- Advertising
- Partnerships
- Giveaways
- Sponsorships
- Public speaking
- Salespeople
- Online reviews
- Organic search, SEO
- Articles
- Radio
- Volunteering, community events
- Industry publications
- Direct mail

- Webinars
- Walk-ins
- Influencer marketing
- Testimonials
- Search and social media paid ads
- Collaborations
- Virtual and in-person events
- Contests

Use this list as a reference, and start executing, to increase your number of new leads.

HOW TO CONVERT MORE LEADS INTO PAYING CLIENTS

There is a saying that "fortune is in the follow up." So often, business owners make one sales attempt, then if there is no response, the prospect never hears from them again. Follow up with your leads regularly and often, at least seven to eleven times before you give up. After that, if you still don't get a response, move them to a different follow-up campaign. You can automate much of this using email marketing automation software like Mailchimp, ActiveCampaign, and Keap (formerly Infusionsoft). Make sure you are following the rules and being SPAM compliant.

Email is not the only way. Use several different touch points to stay in front of your prospects. Here is a non-comprehensive list:

- Email
- Phone calls
- Voicemail drops
- Text messaging
- Direct messaging (Linkedin, Facebook, Instagram)
- Retargeting with paid ads
- Direct mail

- Promotional items
- Invite them to events (virtual and in-person)

You'll want to follow up with any declines, cancels, abandoned carts, etc. and convert them to solid cash.

However, no matter which of the above methods you use, make sure you are delivering valuable information to your prospect and not just selling all the time. According to Gary Vee, a good ratio for content to selling is 3:1—give, give, give, ask—or as Gary says, "Jab, jab, jab, right hook."

HOW TO INCREASE AVERAGE ORDER VALUE

I learned from Verne Harnish, founder of EO, that one often-overlooked strategy for increasing revenue, profitability, and cash, while also improving the perception of your brand, is to raise your prices.

How do you increase prices without causing a big fuss?
- Add more value (upsells and add-ons)
- Clearly illustrate the return on investment
- Offer a guarantee
- Give more, and receive more
- Offer skip-the-line fees
- Offer a VIP service level
- Warranties
- Subscriptions

HOW TO INCREASE REPEAT PURCHASE FREQUENCY

Here are some ways to increase how often your clients or customers come back and shop with you:
- Suggest new and related products to existing clients

- Create a special offer or coupon for existing clients
- Implement a membership or subscription service
- Regularly deliver valuable learning content via email and social media.

BUSINESS PITFALLS TO AVOID

> *"Cash [flow] is the equivalent of financial Valium.*
> *It keeps you cool, calm and collected."*
> —*Bruce Berkowitz (billionaire investor)*

Here are some of the biggest money lessons I've learned through my own failures in business:

Pitfall #1: Not maintaining proper margins.

When our business first crossed the million-dollar-per-year revenue mark, I was ecstatic! But I also wondered, why is there no money in my bank account?

Then when I looked at my profit and loss statement, I realized that we had spent $1,006,000 to earn $1,002,000 in revenue. This means we were $4,000 in the negative.

To make matters worse, we then ended up in a contract dispute with one of our biggest clients. In the end, we prevailed, but the dispute lasted about eight months and added up to about $300,000 in legal fees and lost revenue.

We didn't have any extra money, so to bridge the gap, we had to take out a high-interest loan. To repay the loan, we agreed to let the lender automatically withdraw $300 from our bank account every single business day for about two years. The rest we had to figure out by juggling credit card debt and other small loans. This kept us in a vicious cycle of barely being able to meet payroll and only being able to pay interest on our debts.

We eventually dug our way out of this hole, but had we been operating with proper profit margins, the impact wouldn't have been so lasting.

A lot of business owners think they are making money, when in reality they are losing money. That's one reason 80% of businesses fail within the first five years, and only 5% of businesses make it beyond $1M annual revenue. I see it happen all the time. The business owner assumes that if he buys a blank t-shirt for $2, then puts something on it and sells it for $10, that he made $8 profit. In actuality, once you add up lease payments, utilities, taxes, advertising, labor, merchant fees, insurance, equipment costs, office supplies, materials, ink and thread, meals, travel, etc., and divide that total amount by the number of shirts you make in a year, that one shirt might really cost about $15 to make. It depends on the sales volume, so do this exercise with your real numbers. If it turns out that one shirt is really costing you $15 to make, but you're selling it for $10, then you are actually *losing* $5 on every shirt sale.

Here's how to fix it:

Step 1: Determine your <u>true</u> total cost per average order (TCPAO), by adding up ALL of your expenses.

Step 2: Divide that by the number of units you sell in a year. If you're a service-based business, then your units might be billable hours, houses cleaned, lawns mowed, or cars washed. Figure out the unit that makes most sense for your business.

Step 3: Determine *net profit margin* per average order.

NET PROFIT MARGIN = NET PROFIT / REVENUE

WHERE NET PROFIT = REVENUE – COST

Your net profit margin for every order should be at least 60%. Note that markup is not the same as net profit margin. So to achieve this, multiply the true total cost for that product by at least 2.5 to set your retail price for that product. Using the example above, if the t-shirt costs you $15 to make, you need to sell it for at least $37.50. Round up to $39.99. No one is going to balk at that $1.49.

Pitfall #2: Borrowing money to keep hourly/salary employees paid during slow seasons.

When you're bootstrapping a business (that means growing it organically with no outside funding), time-based pay can be detrimental to your success. We made the mistake of paying people just to show up instead of paying based on results. Then, when our business went through slow periods, we still had to make payroll. If we didn't have the money for payroll, we borrowed it. That was flawed thinking, and a major contributor to the massive debt burden that we once had.

Consider this hypothetical scenario: You take your car to get it washed by hand, and the person washing your car charges by the hour. It personally benefits him more to work slower because then he would earn more money. However, this doesn't necessarily translate into a higher-quality end result. In fact, the person washing your car could be moving slower because he keeps stopping to read personal text messages and scroll through social media.

In contrast, at the car wash down the street that charges a flat rate per vehicle, the workers move much faster because they want to fit in as many vehicles as possible. They also make sure to do an excellent job because they are hungry for five-star reviews.

There is an old adage called Parkinson's Law: work expands to fill the time allotted for its completion. The opposite is also true—work *contracts* to fill the time allotted for its completion. Think about how you completed that huge load of work in a short amount of time the day before your vacation.

For this reason, the hiring small business owner should explore alternatives to time-based pay whenever possible.

Here are some options to consider:
- Fixed price per project
- Performance-based pay – this could be in the form of bonuses that are only activated once certain target numbers are hit
- Pay-per-unit (piecework) – workers are paid X amount per widget produced
- Commission – workers are paid a percentage of the overall order value
- Equity – part or all of the worker's compensation is in the form of company shares; this means they have some ownership in the company
- Phantom stock – similar to equity, but the worker doesn't have true ownership in the company
- Profit sharing – the worker earns a percentage of the company profits (not revenue), usually paid out in dividends at certain times during the year

There are many other options to consider, and you can get creative by combining different incentives. Summary: Pay for results rather than time whenever possible.

Pitfall #3: Always reinvesting everything back into the business

For years, I made the mistake of reinvesting all profits back into the business and paying myself out of what was left over (if anything). I made sure my team was paid, but I would often go without a paycheck.

Then I implemented what I learned in the book *Profit First* by Mike Michalowicz.

The traditional way of thinking is:

REVENUE – EXPENSES = PROFIT

The Profit First method is:

REVENUE – PROFIT = OPERATING EXPENSES

Now what we do is, every day when revenue comes in, we immediately take 10% of that day's revenue and move it to a separate, harder-to-access bank account. This is our Profit Account. By doing this, we guarantee that our business will at least be 10% profitable every year.

Then we take another 10% and move it to a different account, called Owner Pay. By doing this, we make sure that we get a paycheck and can at least feed our family. It turns out eating is good for humans and allows us to be better business owners.

Next, we take 40% and move it to a tax account. This number may be different depending on where you live. By doing this, we make sure that we aren't caught by surprise with a high tax bill. This has happened to us before, and it was not a fun experience.

Lastly, we force ourselves to operate the business with the remaining 40% of revenue. This creates a scarcity effect and stimulates creativity. Instead of just hiring a bunch of people, like we did before, now we look at each problem and think, "How can we automate or streamline this process for the least amount of money possible?"

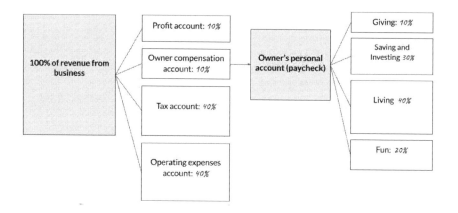

PERSONAL MONEY MANAGEMENT

As you can see from the figure above, we also operate our personal finances with a similar approach:

- 10% is automatically put into a giving account that we use for tithing and charitable donations
- 30% is devoted to saving and investing
- 40% is used for our personal living expenses—mortgage, utilities, groceries, etc.
- 20% is earmarked for fun—travel, gifts, entertainment, etc.

You can adjust your percentages differently, but I suggest following a similar model. For a real-world example using easy math, we will take $10,000/month income and break it down as follows:

- Giving: $1,000/month
- Saving/investing: $3,000/month
- Living expenses: $4,000/month
- Fun: $2,000/month

THE POWER OF COMPOUND INTEREST

"Compound interest is the eighth wonder of the world. He who understands it, earns it . . . he who doesn't, pays it."
—*Albert Einstein*

If you invest $2,000 every month, from age 30 to age 60, assuming an 8% average return on investment, you will have about $3.5M by age 60.

If $2,000 seems daunting, start with $500.

If you invest just $500 every month, from age 25 to age 60, assuming an 8% average return on investment, you will have about $1.4M by age 60.

There are plenty of options for opening online investment accounts. Some that I recommend are E*TRADE, Vanguard, and Acorns.

The key is to start and stay consistent. Make it automated so you can set it and forget it. A great book to read on this subject is *The Automatic Millionaire* by David Bach.

DEBT LEADS TO DEMISE

A few years ago, I was struggling with over $500,000 worth of credit card debt, and I decided I'd had enough. I was stressed out and felt like I could never get ahead. To tackle the problem, I created a spreadsheet listing each account, the total balance, and the interest rate.

I followed the Dave Ramsey approach and paid off the account with the smallest balance first. Doing it this way gives you the quickest psychological win.

Then I attacked the next card and went down the list one by one.

I consolidated the high-interest accounts into no-interest loans and paid them off systematically, until eventually it was all gone.

Now I am debt free, aside from the house I live in. If I can do it, so can you.

> Additional resources: I take you through the exact process, and provide all of the resources needed, in the *From Drowning In Debt to Debt-Free Masterclass*, available at **www.simplesuccess.school**.

MORE PERSONAL FINANCE TIPS

Spend time reviewing your accounts daily. What you measure improves. Use dashboards. Trim unnecessary expenses.

Get rid of ATM cards and debit cards. These make it difficult to track spending, and when your account ends up going negative, the banks charge you fees. Banks know this—that's why they want you to use ATM cards and debit cards.

I haven't personally had an ATM or debit card in over twenty years. Instead, I withdraw enough cash from my account to last an entire month. Then I pay for everything else using one rewards credit card that I pay off in full every month.

Use money management software like Mint or Quicken and review your accounts daily.

Pay off credit cards in full every month; do not carry revolving debt. When it comes to discretionary spending, if you can't afford to pay cash for it, don't buy it.

Keep a budget.

Forced scarcity: Talk to your employer about automatically depositing a portion of your paycheck into your savings account. If you are the business owner, your payroll company can set this up for you and your staff.

If living below your means is difficult for you, then expand your means by adding new income streams.

KEY TAKEAWAYS

- Everyone should own a business—at least a side business, at a minimum—so that you can increase your personal income and take advantage of the tax benefits.
- To grow your business, just a 26% increase in your number of clients, average order value, and average repeat purchase frequency will double your revenue.
- Follow up with clients and prospects often. The fortune is in the follow-up.
- Deliver educational and inspirational content three times more often than you make a direct sales pitch.
- Increase your prices. Calculate the *total* cost per unit and multiply it by at least 2.5 to determine minimum retail price.
- Siphon off a percentage of your revenue FIRST into separate accounts for profits, owner pay, and taxes. Operate your business only using 40% of revenue.
- Compound interest can work for you (investments over time) or against you (debt). Make it work for you.

INSIGHTS

Use this space to write your reflections from this chapter.

What is one insight I learned about myself in regards to my relationship with money?

_____

_____

_____

_____

_____

_____

_____

_____

_____

What is my commitment to action?

_____

_____

_____

_____

_____

_____

_____

_____

CHAPTER 8:
PHYSICAL PRESENCE

"The greatest wealth is health."
—Virgil

"If you're dead you're out of business."
—Gary Vaynerchuk

OVERVIEW

I learned at a young age that your physical body is more malleable than you think. When I was eight years old, I used to go to the YMCA after school. In the locker room, the other boys would laugh at me because my belly button stuck out. They all had "innies"—meaning their belly buttons went in—and I was the only one with an "outty."

I wanted nothing more than to fit in with the rest of my peer group. It was already bad enough that I felt like an outcast. I was a light-skinned Black kid growing up in the 1980s in the South. So I did not fit in with the White kids, and I was also teased by the Black kids, who had browner skin. I was desperate to do whatever it took to fit in, so I would try to change my appearance however I could. It started with my belly button. I asked my mom about it, and she said, "It's fine. Just leave it alone. Some people's belly buttons stick out, and some don't. You are perfectly normal."

I didn't listen to her. At night I would constantly try to push in my belly button, but of course it would just pop right back out. I tried to push it in so often, that it just became an involuntary habit. I'd be watching TV, and my hand would subconsciously be on my belly button trying to push it in, without my even thinking about it. I stopped consciously thinking about it, and just kind of gave up since my mother told me it was impossible, but my subconscious brain did not give up. My fingers kept pushing in my belly button on a daily basis. Then one miraculous day, I remember looking down and realizing that I no longer had an "outty," I now had an "inny" just like the rest of the boys!

This taught me that if I could change my physical appearance, then I can probably change anything in this so-called reality.

Another situation was with my asthma. I remember when I was around ten years old, we had to run a mile in PE class. Most of the kids were finishing in about ten to twelve minutes, but I couldn't finish without having to walk because I would start wheezing and have to use my inhaler. I asked my mom, "How can I make the asthma go away?" She said, "Asthma never goes away. If you have asthma, you have it for your whole life." She's a doctor, and she's my mother, so of course I trust her, and I'm sure that her statement was backed by science.

With exercise-induced asthma, I never played many sports or did anything athletic growing up. I tried to play on the church basketball team, but that didn't go well either because I absolutely sucked. To be honest, I was envious of the football players who were the most popular guys in my school. I was a band/art nerd and voted Most Intellectual. I resented it when I got the Most Intellectual superlative award because I secretly wanted to be Most Popular or Best Dressed or Most Likely to Succeed. But I wasn't in the in-crowd, so I got the nerd award. Other people didn't see it as a bad thing, but at the time I did.

Around the time I hit my mid-twenties, I found myself getting chubby, my hairline was receding, and my eyesight was getting worse. I remember going to my grandfather's funeral, and my wife leaned over and said to me, "This is how you are going to look in a few years," pointing at the pew in front of me, where the next oldest generation of males in my family sat, none of whom were in good shape at the time. Most were chubby or obese, bald or balding, and their clothes hung off of them in a sloppy way. To be fair, we had just lost the patriarch of the family, so everyone was going through a stressful time, and the stress was probably impacting their health and physical appearance, but I didn't yet understand the science behind that. All I know is that my wife's comment sparked something in me to change my body and never go back. She didn't mean anything harmful by her comment; she was just trying to add some comic relief to a sad situation. I knew she would love me regardless of my appearance. I wanted to make the change for myself.

So when I got home, I started running around the neighborhood. It was tough. I would usually have to do a run/walk sequence just to complete a mile or two. My saving grace was my very first iPod because I was able to load audiobooks on it. That way I felt like running wasn't a complete waste of my time because I would be learning new things while I ran.

In addition to that, my older brother Ako had gotten into fitness as well, even though he had the same asthma issues growing up that I had. I don't even remember how it came about, but Ako asked me if I wanted to run the Peachtree Road Race with him. The Peachtree Road Race is a 10K that happens every Fourth of July in Atlanta. The race starts around seven a.m., and there are usually about 60,000 people in attendance. It's the largest 10K in the world.

Now keep in mind, when Ako asked me about this, I was going on thirty years old and could barely run two miles without losing my breath. I would regularly hang out with my friends, drinking until the wee hours of the morning, and on holidays especially, I would sleep in late. On a typical Fourth of July, my modus operandi would be to wake up around noon, start drinking, and get ready to go eat some barbecue somewhere.

So my brother must have been absolutely insane to think that I would wake up at five a.m. on a holiday and go to the busiest street in Atlanta to run with thousands of strangers. But because I am not one to back down from a challenge, I took him up on his offer, and we started training together.

My sheer will and determination to finish that race changed everything. Ako and I ran our first Peachtree together in 2008, just shortly after my thirtieth birthday. It took us an hour to complete it, and we never stopped to walk; we ran the whole way. I was proud of us. Two asthma boys had just run 6.2 miles without a bit of wheezing.

I remember taking my shirt off at the finish line to put on the t-shirt that all finishers get, and you could see in the photo that I was starting to get a little bit of definition around my abs. There I was, thirty years old, and I was starting to finally see some signs of the six-pack that I never had and thought I could never get!

Since then, I have never missed a Peachtree Road Race. The adrenaline rush was indescribable. It felt better than any drug I had ever taken. I would later learn that I actually became addicted to the experience because the pleasure chemicals—dopamine, oxytocin, serotonin, and endorphins—were all released during this experience. Plus, I loved how my body was looking and how I was feeling. I kept running races—half marathons and marathons. The asthma was gone. I was looking younger and less stressed out. I feel like my hair even started growing back a little.

But soon I learned that I really wasn't in as great shape as I thought I was. There are always levels to success. What you see on the outside may not accurately reflect what's happening on the inside. I went for a physical, and the doctor told me that I had high cholesterol. Crap, that sucked.

Then shortly after that, I went to visit my friend Samir Damani, who is a cardiologist in southern California. He had just started a new concierge fitness program for executives, and he let me be an early patient. They put a heart rate monitor around my chest and had me do a VO2 fitness test on a treadmill. I received my fitness score from them, and it was a C on a scale of A–F. I hated getting Cs. Crap, that sucked.

The report also showed that I had excess visceral fat. Visceral fat is the fat around your belly organs, and the doctors explained to me that it is directly linked to heart disease. Crap, that sucked.

This experience taught me that striving to get six-pack abs isn't just a vanity effort; it could also actually save my life. The trainers taught me how to do high-intensity interval training (HIIT) using a heart rate monitor. I had to submit a screenshot of every workout to my trainer.

They instructed me to wear a Fitbit and log a minimum of 10,000 steps per day, every single day. My trainer was watching to make sure I complied.

They taught me the proper macronutrient levels for my protein, carbohydrates, and fat intake. I had to log every meal and report it in the app.

With the proper coaching and accountability, I lost twenty pounds and got down to 9.9% body fat. My cholesterol got back to proper levels. I had more energy than ever, and though I was in my mid-thirties, my body was now more chiseled than ever in my life. I had become a new person, and there was no going back.

If I can do it, then so can you. In the following pages, I will show you how.

THE HIGHEST LEVEL OF CONFIDENCE

Besides the health benefits, why is fitness so important?

If you love how your body looks in its purest form, naked in the mirror, then you have the highest level of confidence.

The reason people buy Lamborghinis, Rolex watches, and designer bags is that it gives them confidence. There's nothing wrong with having these things, but if your confidence is dependent on external objects, then it is only borrowed confidence.

When you love how you look in the mirror naked, that is the highest level of confidence, and you own it. By following the steps in this chapter, you can achieve that level of confidence, and it will radiate into all other areas of your life.

ASSESSMENT

Before we get into the plan, let's first assess your "P" score—your **Physical Presence**. Grade yourself on a scale of 1–10, and remember: You are grading yourself for this particular moment in time—how you're feeling today, right now.

Don't judge your responses. There is no good or bad. Replace self-judgment with curiosity. And be honest. Don't grade yourself aspirationally.

For example, a score of 1 would be: You're hospitalized and incapacitated. You can't breathe, you can barely move, and it feels like you're in constant pain.

In contrast, a score of 10 might mean: You're in the best shape of your life! You could drop what you're doing now and complete a full Ironman with a moment's notice. You're confident in your style, so you love how you look with clothes on. You also have the body of your dreams, so you love how you look naked too! You feel great on the inside, you look great on the outside, and you enter a room with such confidence that people can't help but notice.

So where do you fall on a scale of 1–10? Use space in the companion journal to record your "P" score for today, along with any accompanying thoughts or reflections around your score.

Here are some tips if you're feeling deficient in your physical fitness.

REMINDER: No material in this book is intended to be a substitute for professional medical advice, diagnosis, or treatment. The statements in this book may not be FDA approved. Always seek the advice of your physician or other qualified healthcare provider with any questions you may have regarding a medical condition or treatment, and before undertaking a new health care regimen, and never disregard professional medical advice or delay in seeking it because of something you read in this book, or in any materials mentioned by the author.

STRESS LESS

To win the battle for prime physical presence, you must first recognize the enemy. The number one enemy of health is stress. Stress negatively impacts your sleep, leads to bad eating habits, and releases the hormone cortisol, which increases visceral fat.

Stress ages you faster. Look back at photos of all the United States presidents when they first took office, compared to their last day in office.

For just about every single one of them, their hair turned completely gray or white. This is what happens when you have the most stressful job in the world and the decisions you make affect billions of lives.

So the number one thing you can do to benefit your health is to reduce your stress levels. Refer to the chapter on subconscious restructuring. Gratitude journaling and meditation reduce stress. Also try to avoid toxic people and news headlines.

STAY HYDRATED

Drink lots of water. The U.S. National Academies of Sciences, Engineering, and Medicine determined that an adequate daily fluid intake is about 15.5 cups (3.7 liters) of fluids a day for men, and about 11.5 cups (2.7 liters) of fluids a day for women.

If committing to only water is too much for you and you need some variety, mix it up with other zero-calorie beverages—examples are Coke Zero, black coffee, or unsweet tea—but for best results, stick with just water.

SWEAT DAILY

Another way to combat stress is to increase your capacity to handle it. You do this through vigorous exercise, pushing your heart rate into the highest zones, then allowing it to come back down. Your heart is a muscle, so by pushing your cardiovascular limits, it makes your muscle stronger.

Doing high-intensity interval training (HIIT) three times per week is the best way to get your heart rate up and burn visceral fat. To perform HIIT correctly, wear a heart rate monitor (it can be a smart watch), and use an app like iCardio to monitor your workout.

You can do HIIT with pretty much any cardio exercise; I find running to be the most straightforward.

I recommend doing a fitness assessment in iCardio to determine your heart rate zones. For a crude estimate of your maximum age-related heart rate, subtract your age from 220. So if you're 40 years old, your maximum heart rate is likely around 180 beats per minute (BPM).

This means for a forty-year-old, your heart rate zones may be something like this example (this can be a little different for everyone):

Zone 5	170-180 BPM	All-out sprinting
Zone 4	160-169 BPM	Race-pace running
Zone 3	150-159 BPM	Running
Zone 2	140-149 BPM	Jogging
Zone 1	130-139 BPM	Speed walking

Start running at a warmup pace for ten minutes in Zone 2 or 3, then go all out, up to Zone 5. Stay in Zone 5 for 60 seconds. If you are doing it right, it will feel pretty brutal, like your heart is about to beat out of your chest.

After 60 seconds in Zone 5, return to a walk, and let your HR descend to Zone 1. Then repeat this cycle 3–5 times. Do this 2–3 times per week on alternating days.

A cool benefit of HIIT is that your body continues to burn calories up to sixteen hours after your workout because of a phenomenon called excess post-exercise oxygen consumption (EPOC). That is why you should not do HIIT every single day, but only about three times per week, allowing your body time to recover in between sessions.

SUPPLEMENTS

Keep your immune system strong with Vitamin C, zinc, probiotics, fish oil, and multivitamins. Refer to the bottle for dosage instructions.

I only deviate from this with Vitamin C. I typically take 6000mg every day—3000mg in the morning and 3000mg in the evening.

Visit 6packmindset.com for more supplements that I use.

SNACK, AND USE SMALLER PLATES

Instead of filling up twelve-inch platters and eating three times per day, buy six-inch paper plates and only eat whatever you can fit on the plate. Eat portions this size about six times per day. This signals to your body that it doesn't need to store fat because it will learn that more food is coming in the next couple of hours.

SHIFT YOUR CALORIES TO THE BEGINNING OF THE DAY

Experts weigh in differently on this, but I believe it is better to shift the majority of your caloric intake to the earlier part of your day. I've noticed that I drop weight faster when I make this shift. My theory is that this gives you more time to digest and burn off the calories as you move around throughout the day. "Eat breakfast like a king, lunch like a prince, and dinner like a pauper." —Adelle Davis

SKIP THE BEIGE

Try making every plate more colorful and less beige. Beige foods are bread, cake, bagels, fried foods, chips, potatoes, etc. Replace that with colorful fruit, fish, meats, legumes, berries, peppers, and leafy greens. Try removing all beige from your diet for thirty days and see how you feel.

STEPS

Use a pedometer like Fitbit, and get in at least 10,000 steps per day, every day.

SIXTY/TWENTY/TWENTY

To drop fat and build muscle quickly, aim for a daily macronutrient breakdown of 60% protein, 20% carbs, and 20% fat. Log your meals in an app like MyFitnessPal so that you can see your daily macro breakdown. That which gets measured improves.

Note: you only want to try a super-high protein diet for short stints at a time, like thirty days. You also want to be mindful about the type of protein you ingest and be mindful of your cholesterol.

If your goal is not losing fat and building muscle, then a different macronutrient breakdown may better suit your goals.

SWITCH IT UP

Vary your cardio exercises. Swim, bike, run, jump rope, trail running, speed work, etc. All of the different exercises work different muscle groups.

STRENGTH TRAINING

Cardio is a must, but it is important to lift weights and push your muscles daily too, even if it's just body weight, like pull-ups and push-ups. We lose testosterone as we age, and strength training can help keep testosterone levels high.

People think of testosterone as a male hormone, but according to Medical News Today, low testosterone can also cause one or more of the following symptoms in women:

- sluggishness
- muscle weakness
- fatigue
- sleep disturbances
- reduced sex drive
- decreased sexual satisfaction
- weight gain
- fertility issues

SUNSHINE

Step outside and get a daily dose of sunshine! The sun provides Vitamin D, which boosts your mood and your immune system. Sometimes nothing feels better than fresh air and a sun-kissed glow. Exercise outdoors if you can. Just remember sunscreen because unprotected sun exposure also ages your skin.

STAND MORE, SIT LESS

Dr. James Levine, director of Mayo Clinic at Arizona State University, coined the popular phrase "sitting is the new smoking" because, according to some research, sitting for extended periods of time can increase your risk of developing chronic health problems like heart disease, diabetes, and certain cancers.[10]

To combat this, get a standing desk and stand up while you work. Invest in a slow-moving treadmill under your desk so you can walk while working.

Take breaks and get up from your seat. Move around more. Take walking meetings whenever possible.

STRETCH OFTEN

As we age, we lose our flexibility. Being intentional about stretching and focusing on your mobility has several benefits:

- helps manage stress
- reduces tension
- enhances relaxation
- decreases muscle stiffness
- increases range of motion
- reduces risk of injury
- relieves post-exercise aches and pains
- improves posture

SIGN UP FOR RACES AND "SHIRT-OFF" EVENTS

This is a mental trick that I use several times a year. I will pre-register for events where I know there is a likelihood of me ending up shirtless in

---

[10] "The dangers of sitting: why sitting is the new smoking," *Better Health Channel*, https://www.betterhealth.vic.gov.au/health/healthyliving/the-dangers-of-sitting

photos. I don't want to feel embarrassed with my shirt off, so I strive hard to get in optimal shape before each event.

When I have a date on my calendar that I'm looking forward to, it makes me push even harder toward my fitness goal because now I have an immediate purpose. The mission becomes clear and real, and there's no turning back.

Ladies can use this mental trick too. Instead of being topless, it may mean wearing a two-piece swimsuit or a sports bra.

Here are some examples of events you can use as motivational milestones throughout the year:

- A beach vacation
- A pool party
- A photo shoot
- A retreat
- A boat trip
- A race
- A rave
- A festival
- A physique competition

SEX MORE OFTEN

Not only is sex great exercise, but when you orgasm your body releases the pleasure chemical dopamine, as well as endorphins and oxytocin. These feel-good hormones activate pleasure centers in the brain that create feelings of intimacy and relaxation. This reduces stress and anxiety, and therefore reduces cortisol levels.

SLEEP WELL

Over the past several decades, the amount of time that Americans spend sleeping has steadily decreased, as well as the self-reported quality of that sleep. During the same period, the average body mass index (BMI) of Americans has increased. Much research points to correlation between the two. According to one study of seniors aged 67 to 99, those who slept five or fewer hours per night were three times as likely to develop obesity than those who slept seven to eight hours each night.[11]

Here are some reasons why quality sleep can help with weight loss, as I've learned through research, personal experience, and conversations with my friend Dr. Michael Breus, also known as "The Sleep Doctor":

The longer you're awake, the more likely you are to eat . . . and you'll usually crave foods higher in salt, sugar, fat, carbohydrates, and calories.

Studies have shown that sleep deprivation causes your body to secrete more cortisol during the day, perhaps in an effort to keep you awake.[12] Cortisol is the stress-response hormone. More of it in your body leads to more belly fat and a weaker immune system.

Sleeping less may disrupt circadian rhythms. Less cortisol is secreted during the deeper sleep cycles.[13]

You lose water weight through breathing and sweating while you sleep.[14]

---

[11] "Can You Lose Weight Overnight?" *Healthline*, https://www.healthline.com/nutrition/how-to-lose-weight-overnight

[12] Leproult R, Copinschi G, Buxton O, Van Cauter E. "Sleep loss results in an elevation of cortisol levels the next evening." *Sleep*. 1997 Oct;20(10):865-70. PMID: 9415946.

[13] "How to remove cortisol from the body naturally," Medical News Today, https://www.medicalnewstoday.com/articles/322335

[14] "Do you lose weight during sleep?," *Medical News Today*, https://www.medicalnewstoday.com/articles/do-you-lose-weight-when-you-sleep

Usually the less you sleep, the less energy you have for exercise and physical activity. And if you aren't exercising, you aren't burning the calories to lose weight.[15]

In my experience, not only does sleep help you lose weight, but you also think clearer and look younger when you are well rested.

From all of my research and experimentation, I've narrowed it down to these twenty things that actually work to promote quality sleep:

- Dark room – I use blackout window curtains
- Eye mask
- Cold room – I keep the thermostat on 70 or lower during the night
- Breathable pajamas
- Breathable sheets
- Heavy comforter/blanket
- White noise – I use a bedroom fan. Sometimes, I'll use soundscapes (Audible has several good free ones included with the Premium Plus level). Also, the Sleep Cycle app has some good built-in sleep aids.
- Sex – boosts oxytocin (the pleasure/connection hormone) and reduces cortisol (the stress hormone), thereby helping you sleep. Added bonus from sex: a good core workout!
- Ear plugs – I prefer Putty Buddies
- Eat a light, high-protein snack before bed so I don't wake up hungry in the middle of the night.
- Don't exercise too late in the day. If I have to do an evening workout, I make sure to be done and showered at least four hours before bedtime.
- Get lots of sun exposure throughout the day.
- Avoid caffeine and energy-boosting supplements after two p.m.

---

[15] "Diet and Exercise and Sleep," *Sleep Foundation*, December 4, 2020, https://www.sleepfoundation.org/physical-health/diet-exercise-sleep

- Write out my to-do list/brain dump for the next day. Get it out of my head so it doesn't keep me up.
- Gratitude journal
- Blue-blocker glasses – I own the TrueDark Elite Boxed Set. Wear the gold lenses at sunset, then switch to the red lenses an hour before bed.
- Meditate right before lights out
- Sometimes I'll watch a non-fiction show or read a book (while wearing my red lens blue blockers) to take my mind off of work or anything that may be concerning me. Something not too heavy that I can fall asleep watching/reading.
- If I do wake up in the middle of the night, I don't count the hours, or judge myself. I don't lie in bed awake. I just get up and do something (while wearing my red lens blue blockers).
- Last resort (consult your doctor first) – over-the-counter sleep aids. Sometimes I'll take half a dose of ZzzQuil and two capsules of Acetaminophen PM 500mg.
- Last, last, last resort (consult your doctor first)—prescription sleep meds or anxiety meds. For some people the side effects and addictive qualities of prescription sleep meds can be very, very dangerous . . . but sleep deprivation is very dangerous too. If none of the other methods work for you, then talk to your doctor about prescription sleep meds, but be sure to express your concern about forming a dependency on the medication.

FORMING NEW HABITS

If you have trouble motivating yourself to work out, here's a quick life hack for you: When you're preparing for bed, put your alarm clock in your workout shoes and place your shoes by the door. Sleep in your workout clothes. When your alarm sounds and you get up to turn it off, you're already up, with your workout clothes on, standing over your shoes. May as well work out.

The key to making the above habits stick is to do them routinely and quickly figure out the reward so you get that dopamine hit and want to do it again. Overcome the boredom of exercise by making it fun.

Tie things you enjoy doing to exercise. If you're social, try group activities like intramural sports. If you like video games, explore the fitness games on Nintendo Switch and Oculus Quest. If you like learning, listen to audio books while exercising. Like new music? Explore new Spotify stations while exercising. Like conversations? Listen to podcasts while exercising. Movies and TV? Binge watch Netflix while on the treadmill, bike, or rower.

It's hard for me even to believe it about myself, but I am now addicted to fitness. When I don't work out, I feel grumpy and irritable. We'll go deep on forming beneficial addictions later in this book.

Another great book to read on this subject is *Atomic Habits* by James Clear.

HOW TO UPGRADE YOUR WARDROBE AND STYLE

Physical presence is about more than just fitness and nutrition. It's about your overall appearance and how you groom, dress, and carry yourself.

Fashion is temporary and expensive.

Style is timeless and affordable.

The number one thing most people can do to look more stylish and sophisticated is wear clothes that fit well and are tailored to their measurements. As far as knowing what to wear, here's a simple hack: find the most recent issue of a style magazine, like *GQ* or *Elle*, and just copy a style that you like.

Hire a stylist or a personal shopper to help you—it's more affordable than you might think.

The same thing applies to your grooming and hair. Go to a professional.

When you invest in your look, it pays back tenfold. You'll attract more awesomeness, carry yourself with more confidence, and close more deals.

KEY TAKEAWAYS

- Your physical body is more malleable than you think.
- Stress is the #1 enemy of physical wellness.
- Eat colorful meals on smaller plates.
- Do HIIT three times per week.
- Sleep is vital to your health.
- Invest in experts to help you find the right look so that you always look good and feel good about yourself.

INSIGHTS

Use this space to write your reflections from this chapter.

What is one insight I learned about myself in regards to my physical presence?

_____

_____

_____

_____

_____

_____

_____

_____

_____

_____

What is my commitment to action?

_____

_____

_____

_____

_____

_____

_____

_____

_____

_____

CHAPTER 9:
LOVE & LEADERSHIP

"Love creates a communion with life. Love expands us, connects us, sweetens us, ennobles us. Love springs up in tender concern, it blossoms into caring action. It makes beauty out of all we touch. In any moment we can step beyond our small self and embrace each other as beloved parts of a whole."
—*Jack Kornfield*

OVERVIEW

The Love & Leadership category has to do not only with your relationships but also your contribution to the world, your purpose, the causes you support.

Wherever there is an exchange of time and/or money, there is a relationship. We have a relationship with our spouses, with our children, our business partners, with clients and customers, with our audiences.

You're reading this book right now, so you and I have a relationship because I spent time writing it and you have exchanged your time and money to learn the knowledge that I have to share.

THE 6 TYPES OF INTERPERSONAL RELATIONSHIPS

There 6 types of interpersonal relationships are:

- Acquaintanceships
- Platonic
- Friendships
- Romantic
- Family
- Professional

Some people may fall into more than one of these categories in your life or transition from one category to another.

THE 5 STAGES OF A RELATIONSHIP

With each person, there are five stages that every relationship goes through, according to psychologist George Levinger:

- Acquaintance
- Build-up
- Continuation
- Deterioration
- Ending

We consider successful relationships to be the ones that get to the Continuation stage and stay there.

But some relationships are meant to be temporary. The key is determining the relationships that matter and keeping them in the Continuation phase. This is done through nurturing.

ESCALATING AND NURTURING

Any relationship that you either want to escalate from one type to another or keep in the continuance phase likely requires nurturing.

For example, when I was a freshman in college, I crossed paths with an upperclassman sorority girl named Monica. We exchanged names and realized that we had some mutual friends, but we didn't exchange any contact information. I figured she was out of my league anyway, so we remained acquaintances.

A few weeks later I found out Monica and her roommate were having a house party, so I went with my friend Chris. When I got to the party, Monica and I talked to each other for hours, literally. Although we hit it off well, there was nothing romantic about it because she made it very clear that she had a boyfriend and there were pictures of him everywhere. We exchanged phone numbers, though, so in my mind, we had entered the Build-up phase, and our relationship type escalated from Acquaintanceship to Platonic.

Monica graduated and moved to Atlanta. She had landed a good job as an insurance broker, and she had a townhouse in the city. I was still in school about ninety minutes away in Athens. Our relationship was still just Platonic, but I would call her about once or twice a month just to talk. She still showed very little romantic interest but would entertain my conversations.

This rhythm lasted about two years, and we got to know each other pretty well. She even called me a couple of times to check on me, when she heard about some of the dumb mishaps I encountered—like getting arrested and getting suspended from school—that I mentioned earlier in this book. I would say that we lightly transitioned from Platonic to Friendship during those two years.

I, of course, left an open invitation for Monica to come visit me whenever she happened to be in Athens visiting her sorority sisters. To my surprise, one day she called and said, "Hey, I'm in town! What are you up to? Where do you live?" I gave her directions, and when I opened the door to greet her, I could tell there was a different look in her eye. Something gave me the sense that we were about to escalate from Friendship to Romantic.

As it turns out, she had broken up with her boyfriend, and I was right. I guess my nurturing paid off. Even though I was still a broke, wild college kid who made bad choices and she was a level-headed young woman working in corporate America, I guess she saw something in me. It also helped that she was familiar with me because of our regular phone calls.

Tip: Consistency, frequency, and familiarity over time builds trust. This applies to sales and marketing too.

Monica and I started dating and later started a business together. Over twenty years later, we are still married, have multiple businesses together, and have two amazing kids. This is a rare example of how one relationship can move through all of the different types—from Acquaintanceship to Platonic to Friendship to Romantic, then add on Professional and Family too.

A NOTE ABOUT KIDS

Raising children is a complex subject deserving of its own book—several books, in fact. Raising kids is joyful, but it can also put a strain on the parents' relationship with each other. I do not claim to be the perfect parent, but my kids think I'm awesome, and I think they are awesome too.

Here are some quick lessons that I've learned from my adventures as a parent so far:

Before having kids, I thought I had no free time. After having kids, I realized that I actually had an abundance of free time before kids.

I used to complain about waking up in the middle of the night to feed a baby or change a diaper, until I viewed things through a different lens and realized that once the diaper days are over, I will never get that time back with them again. This taught me to appreciate those moments.

Having kids made me want to earn more, do better in life, and become a better person. I wanted to be someone they look up to.

It feels like every thirty days your kid changes—he has grown, has a different interest, or does/says something new. Appreciate every moment because it changes so fast.

Time flies, and before we know it our kids will be adults. My wife and I are intentional about prioritizing each other in our own relationship. We have shared interests outside of the kids, so that when we are empty-nesters we still know and like each other.

ASSESSMENT

Now let's assess your "L" score for how you rank your **Love & Leadership** area of life. These are your different types of relationships. Grade yourself on a scale of 1–10, and remember:

You are grading yourself for this particular moment in time—how you're feeling today, right now. Don't judge your responses. There is no good or bad. Replace self-judgment with curiosity. And be honest. Don't grade yourself aspirationally.

For your "L" area, a score of 1 might mean: you feel lonely and dejected. You crave relationships with others, but nothing seems to last.

In contrast, a score of 10 might mean: You're surrounded by people who love and respect you. Your friendships, relationships with coworkers, family life, and romantic relationships are all thriving. Or maybe you enjoy being alone and you want to stay that way. Either way, if you are completely happy in the area of your love, leadership, and relationships with others, then give yourself a 10 out of 10.

So where do you fall on a scale of 1–10? Use space in the companion journal to record your "L" score for today, along with any accompanying thoughts or reflections around your score.

HOW TO NURTURE RELATIONSHIPS

How do you nurture these relationships? Consider *The 5 Love Languages*®, designed by Gary Chapman. The 5 Love Languages were originally designed for romantic relationships, but they can be modified and applied to all of the different relationship types.

The 5 Love Languages are how someone prefers to express and receive love. They are:

- Words of affirmation
- Quality time
- Physical touch
- Acts of service
- Receiving gifts

You can take the quiz determine your love language and find tons of additional resources at www.5lovelanguages.com.

Consider having your friends, your kids, your significant other take the assessment too. Share your results with each of them.

I do not receive anything for promoting The 5 Love Languages; I just endorse the model because it works.

NURTURING TRANSCENDS ALL DIMENSIONS

One thing I hope you are starting to notice about each of the six dimensions of life is that every one of them needs nurturing if you want them to continue in a positive way.

We need to consistently and daily nurture our subconscious restructuring.

We need to consistently nurture our intelligence.

We need to consistently nurture our income. Make sure you do some small tweak daily that increases your income and or decreases your outflow.

If you're an employer, you need to nurture your relationships with your clients, prospects, and team members on a consistent basis.

We need to constantly nurture our physical presence by working out daily and eating right.

We need to constantly nurture our relationships with family members, with our spouses, and our kids. If you're dating, you need to nurture your relationships with your potential suitors and people that you meet.

And you need to consistently prime the pump to fuel your soul with awesome new experiences and memories to maximize your brief time here on this Earth.

LEADERSHIP AND CORE VALUES

Early in my entrepreneurial years, I was a terrible manager. Our company had a poor culture, and this resulted in high employee turnover.

Through my entrepreneur mentors and a plethora of business books, I learned the importance of implementing Core Values in our company. The Core Values are the guiding principles of a company, which steer the company culture and act as the framework for every decision that needs to be made—from hiring and firing to how to prioritize orders.

You've probably seen Core Values before—those words that are plastered on the walls of some companies' headquarters. The immature, inexperienced Ethan thought this was a corny and pointless thing to do, until some friends of mine who were running much larger businesses than mine told me that implementing Core Values was a main factor in growing their businesses to multiple millions in revenue.

So we sat down with the A-players on our team and listed out all of their winning qualities one by one. Then we cross-referenced this list with five-star reviews that we received from customers and pulled out some of the words that we saw repeated. Then we narrowed down the list to these phrases:

PROMISES—We do what we say, like the sun rises each day. In other words, we honor our commitments, stated or implied.

ACCURACY—We never skimp on precision. We make exactly what the client envisioned.

LOGIC & LEARNING—When faced with complex challenges, we use logic and experience to get to "Yes."

SYSTEMS—We follow existing processes, document new processes, and continuously improve processes. If systems only live in your head, then team-wide consistency is dead.

POSITIVE & ENGAGED—We're happy about work, and our work makes us happy.

NO-SILOS—Every team member always considers how their individual actions affect the big picture. No tunnel vision and just thinking about yourself.

ACTION-ORIENTED SELF-STARTERS—If it aligns with the Core Values, don't ask permission. Just do it and fulfill the mission.

NO EXCUSES—A poem that I had to internalize during my fraternity pledging experience was, "Excuses are tools of the incompetent. They build monuments of nothingness. Those who choose to use them seldom amount to anything." We recite this and the other Core Values during our team huddles.

This is the code that we live by.

What does this have to do with relationships? While this is a business example, any group or team relationship—even your family—can benefit from having documented Core Values. This sets clear expectations and removes all ambiguity.

Once you've established Core Values for your team, group, company, or family, post them everywhere. Print them on wearable items. Weave the values into routine company activities such as interviews, onboarding, meetings, quarterly reviews, and company literature.

You can see an example video of our Core Values in action by visiting **www.zeuscloset.com** and clicking on the Career Opportunities link.

COMMANDING VS. INSPIRING

I learned so much during my term as president of an Entrepreneurs' Organization (EO) chapter. EO is a non-profit support network for business owners founded in 1987. There are about 15,000 members worldwide, across nearly 70 different countries, at the time of this writing. The minimum requirement to join is that you must own a $1M/year revenue business.[16]

Being elected chapter president means that you direct a board of volunteer member-leaders, who also happen to be busy managing their own businesses and families. The time demand of each board role can be as much as a part-time job, but the board members receive no financial compensation.

I served as president of the Atlanta chapter, which at the time, had about 150 members, 30 of whom were board members.

So how do you make a group of 30 busy, independent bosses do what you need them to do, when there's no paycheck to dangle over their heads?

You don't *make* them do anything. You *inspire* them.

I knew that the way to succeed was to communicate a grand vision for the future of the chapter. A vision where we all benefit once it is accomplished. A vision where every member feels as though she is receiving ten times the value of her membership dues in return.

This inspired the board to accomplish some amazing feats, exceeding every metric that we set as a goal. We broke records and won awards at EO's Global Leadership Conference. More importantly, we helped improve the lives and businesses of many entrepreneurs.

---

[16] Entrepreneurs' Organization, https://eonetwork.org

As board members invested their time to help make the vision real, I thanked them profusely. I created unique experiences for them throughout the year and surprised them with gifts. Remember, these were *volunteers*.

Then I had an "Aha!" moment—I should treat my employees like volunteers too.

Even though I could fire them at any time, they really are not obligated to work for me. They could earn a comparable income anywhere else. So I learned to treat my team members like volunteers—with utmost respect, always showing appreciation, nurturing them, and leading them through inspiration.

As a leader, you can inspire people or you can command people. You can either make people do what you want, or you can inspire them to want to do it on their own. Inspiring people is more effective because then they *want* to be all-in, for the collective good.

EXERCISES

For your action item, write down the ten people with whom you interact the most.

Have them take the 5 Love Languages quiz and share your results with each other.

Over the next thirty days, make a point to express your love to each of those people in *their* love language (not yours).

KEY TAKEAWAYS

- Elevating a relationship to the next level requires action, intentionality, and nurturing.
- Keeping a relationship in the Continuance phase requires nurturing the relationship in the other person's Love Language, and vice versa.
- The benefit of nurturing relationships transcends all six dimensions of life.
- Inspiring others is a more effective form of leadership than commanding others.

INSIGHTS

Use this space to write your reflections from this chapter.

What are some insights I learned about myself in regards to my relationships? Social relationships? Romantic relationships? Family relationships? Professional relationships?

_____

_____

_____

_____

_____

_____

_____

_____

_____

_____

What is my commitment to action?

_____

_____

_____

_____

_____

_____

_____

_____

_____

_____

CHAPTER 10:
ENTERTAINING EXPERIENCES

"Life is about creating and living experiences that are worth sharing."
—Steve Jobs

OVERVIEW

Believe it or not, it is possible to have it all in every other area of life yet be completely bored, even depressed. The way you counter this is to deliberately pursue new, entertaining experiences. What good is it to work hard if you don't have the freedom of time, and the intentionality, to enjoy the fruits of your labor?

I remember when our business started doing really well, we were able to buy a new house and furnish it with all of the coolest furniture and features. When my mom came over, she congratulated me and told me how proud she was, but I remember being so tired from working in my business that I had no free time actually to *enjoy* all of the stuff. There was one room in particular that I decorated with all of the latest flat-screen TVs, built-in surround sound, movie theater chairs, and entertainment tech. It was like my man cave, with all black walls and furniture, so I call it the Black Room. But I realized after almost a whole year went by that I had spent zero time in the Black Room.

This experience taught me 3 lessons for happiness:

1. Memories > material items
2. Freedom > money
3. Now > later

Then later, at a conference, I met Jesse Itzler—founder of Marquis Jet and husband to billionaire Sara Blakely—where he introduced a concept called a "f*** it list."

I had heard of a bucket list before, but the idea never really moved me because it is a list of all the things you want to do before you die. To me, a bucket list seemed like something only old people do, and I never want to feel old. Plus, what happens when I finish my bucket list? Do I then "kick the bucket"?

Instead, a "f*** it list," as I remember it, is any wild and crazy thing that you were going to put off until later in life, or until you reach a certain income level, or until X happens—but instead you say "f*** it" and do it *now.*

This concept is something that I planted in my subconscious, and it inspired many of the pivotal decisions that I've made—like running for EO president before I felt ready, traveling alone to Antarctica during a busy time in my business (more on this later), speaking on stages despite having imposter syndrome . . . even writing this book.

Who cares if you're not ready?

You'll probably never be ready.

F*** it. Do it now. Tomorrow isn't promised.

ASSESSMENT

So let's assess your "E" score. How would you rank the quality and quantity of **Entertaining Experiences** in your life?

Grade yourself on a scale of 1–10, and remember: You are grading yourself for this particular moment in time—how you're feeling today, right now. Don't judge your response. There is no good or bad. Replace self-judgment with curiosity. And be honest. Don't grade yourself aspirationally.

Here are some examples:

For your "E" area, a score of 1 might mean you are completely bored with life. You want to experience new things, but something keeps holding you back. It's been a long time since you experienced something new.

In contrast, a score of 10 might mean you check stuff off your bucket list (or you f**** it list) before breakfast! You are always traveling to new places and trying new things. Your life is full of excitement because no two days are the same!

So where do you fall on a scale of 1–10? Use space in the companion journal to record your "E" score for today, along with any accompanying thoughts or reflections around your score.

YOUR VISION MATRIX™

To help you improve this area, we are going to create a visualization tool that I call your Vision Matrix™.

Step 1: Draw a grid forming six boxes on a piece of paper. In each box, write the words: DO, BE, HAVE/KEEP, LEARN, CHANGE, GIVE.

DO	BE
HAVE/KEEP	LEARN
CHANGE	GIVE

Step 2: Take ten minutes and write things in each box. You don't have to go in order. Just write what comes to your mind and put it in the corresponding area. Let the pen keep flowing. Don't judge your desires or worry about what anyone else might think. It is important to do this exercise quickly so that the words flow from your subconscious.

Play some instrumental music that inspires you and pour yourself a glass of a beverage that relaxes you. This exercise is meant to be fun and free flowing.

What are some things you want to DO in life? For example, visit every Wonder of the World? Do an ayahuasca retreat? Go skydiving? Let your imagination run wild. Write everything that comes to your mind in the "DO" box.

When I was thirty-eight years old, I decided that I wanted to visit all seven continents before my fortieth birthday. At the time, I had only been to four continents—North America, Europe, Asia, and Africa—so I only had a small window of time to squeeze in the other three.

That same year, I attended a conference in Hyderabad, India, where we enjoyed once-in-a-lifetime experiences like exclusive dinners in palaces. In fact, I enjoyed a fourteen-course meal at the world's largest dining table, with over 100 other entrepreneurs from around the world. On the return flight home, instead of flying back the way I came, I decided to circumnavigate the globe and enjoy extended layovers in Bangkok, Singapore, Australia, and South Korea. Five continents down.

Then when I was thirty-nine, I embarked on a two-week voyage through South America, with the plan for the trip to culminate in a flight from Punta Arenas, the southernmost city in South America, to the northern tip of Antarctica. I am not a fan of cold weather or long boat trips, so I sought out the fastest route to Antarctica, just so I could check the box.

Unfortunately, flights to Antarctica can be very risky, and foggy, windy weather prohibited my flight from happening. While I was disappointed by the fact that I didn't make it to the seventh continent at that time, I trust God's will and am thankful that I made it back home to my family safely. I also had countless unforgettable experiences during my two weeks traveling through Chile and Peru.

This experience reminded me of two things:

Despite my greatest plans, some things are out of my control, like the weather or a pandemic, and

Many times in life, the journey *is* the destination.

I have no regrets, and I continue to fill my "DO" bucket daily.

Relinquish your attachment to the outcome. Just continue to write things in your "DO" box.

Next, what are some things you want to BE? For example, a bestselling author? A movie star? A billionaire? Think in terms of titles. What are some ways you want others to describe you? She's a _____. He's a _____. Write as many words as possible in the "BE" box.

What are some things you want to HAVE (or keep)? These can be material items. A private jet? Your own island? A fleet of exotic cars? Or it could be that you want to have more children. Or you want to have peace. Or you want six-pack abs. Write down anything you want to HAVE in this box.

What are some things you want to LEARN? A new language? How to fly a plane? How to code an app? Write down anything you want to learn in life in this box.

What are some things you want to CHANGE? About yourself, about your community, about the world. Write any changes that you want to make in this box.

What are some things you want to GIVE? Maybe you have a goal of donating a million dollars to your favorite charity. Or building a school in a developing country. Or maybe you want to share your knowledge with others by giving it away and teaching others. Write everything that comes to mind in the "GIVE" box.

Once you have written for ten minutes, stop and continue to the next exercise.

YOUR VISION MOVIE™

Now open your favorite search engine and click on the Images tab. Search for every term that you wrote down in the exercise above. Find an image that best represents each goal and save it to an album or folder on your device.

Ideally, you should end up with a folder of about twenty to thirty images.

On most devices, you can press the Share button or Play button, and you should be presented with an option to generate a slideshow of your images. If you want to get more elaborate, you can edit them in a video editing app or send it to an editor on Fiverr.com.

The goal is to create a video with moving images. Use the Ken Burns effect to pan still images so that it feels like a motion picture.

This is your Vision Movie™, and I want you to watch it as much as possible, every day.

You can also print the images and create a vision board, but there is something about moving images that tricks your brain into feeling the emotion and making it real.

Think about a time that you sat in a movie and shed a tear because you were overwhelmed with emotion. Logic says the movie isn't real, but your brain doesn't know the difference. It feels the emotion and can produce real, physical reactions in your body as a response to what you are watching.

What we are doing here is using NLP (neuro-linguistic programming) to trick your brain into normalizing the things that you want to manifest in your life. The repetition and immersion causes your brain to perceive the scenes in your movie as already being real, so your subconscious will lead you to take the right actions and make the right micro-decisions and macro-decisions, which will ultimately lead to your Vision Movie™ becoming your new reality. When it happens, it feels like it's just magic, but it is actually scientific.

"The thing about beliefs is they are like a program that keeps running, where you keep checking things against whether it matches your beliefs or not," says Dr. Richard Bandler, co-creator of NLP. "And when your beliefs say that things are possible, and things will make you feel good, then what's going to happen is it is going to affect you physiologically in a very different way than if you believe it's impossible. When you believe that things are impossible, you do not actually try, and you certainly do not try with every fiber in your soul and every cell in your body."

Repeat the process above to update your Vision Movie™ regularly. As you continue to evolve in life, you will accomplish things on your list, and you will also think of new experiences that your soul desires. Your Vision Movie™ is not static; it is an ever-changing, dynamic, living thing, and it should be treated as such.

OTHER VISUALIZATION PLACEMENTS

Vision boards – post copies of it on your bathroom mirror, in your closet, and on your nightstand, so it is the first thing you see when you wake up and the last thing you see before you go to sleep.

Smart watch faces – You can program your Apple Watch to use photos from your vision album as the face background.

Screensavers – you can pull from your vision album for photo screensavers on computers and TVs

Computer desktop wallpaper

Phone wallpaper

The key is total immersion. You want to see these images everywhere so that they are seared into your subconscious. Your brain will normalize them and will work to synchronize opportunities in the universe with your subconscious and conscious decisions, which ultimately makes your visions a reality.

APPEAL TO THE SENSES

Another key is to communicate with your subconscious through the five representational systems:

- Visual (sight)
- Auditory (sound)
- Olfactory (smell)
- Gustatory (taste)
- Kinesthetic (physical movement/touch)

Doing this requires going beyond just the Vision Movie™. For example, if there's a dream car you want, go to the dealership and sit in it.

- See how it shines.
- Hear the engine roar.
- Smell the leather.
- Lick the steering wheel (okay, maybe not).
- Feel how it handles the road.

Video record the experience and add it to your Vision Movie™. Even though you can't record tastes and smells, the recording playback will remind your brain of the experience.

THE VISION MOVIE™ AT WORK

There have been so many times in my life when scenes from my Vision Movie™ have manifested in real life that I can't possibly recount all of them here.

For example, the pool and oasis that I have in my backyard were once just a picture on my vision board (this is before I developed the concept of a Vision Movie™).

Another example is when my wife put an image of her dream car on her vision board. We aren't huge car fanatics or anything, but we test drove a Tesla and she immediately fell in love with it. At the time, it was way out of our budget, and we weren't even in the market for a new car. So I added it to my Vision Movie™ with a "one day in the future" type of expectation.

As fate would have it, six months later, my wife's car wouldn't start and she needed to pick up the kids. This caused me anxiety because, at the time, we were a one-car household, and I felt it was my responsibility to make sure my family had a safe, reliable vehicle. When I researched the safest cars, it just so happened that year that the Tesla Model S topped the list of safest cars by the National Highway Traffic Safety Administration (NHTSA).

Still believing it was out of my budget, I tried my luck anyway and did a few searches to see if maybe we could find a pre-owned Tesla that made sense. I ran across a listing that seemed to be priced ridiculously low, but the car looked great, so I put a contract down to hold it. Everything checked out, and the car was like brand new. All we needed to do was close the deal.

But then there was radio silence.

We didn't hear back from the selling company for several days, and they weren't responding to our emails. When they finally replied, they said that the price was listed incorrectly. What a letdown.

I reminded them that we did nothing wrong, and the car was already under contract, so they should honor it. Another two days of silence went by, and they finally said "yes."

Just like that, we were driving off the lot with her dream car, only six months after manifesting it. A short time later, we paid it off early.

This stuff is real, and it works.

One lesson I learned from this experience is never to put time constraints on my requests from the universe.

Another lesson I learned is to never force *how* something is manifested in your life. You just state what you want, and let the universe worry about how. It will open doors and pathways you could never have imagined.

An example is when I really wanted to get my body in top physical shape. I looked up pictures of guys with six-pack abs, eight-pack abs, etc., to include in my Vision Movie™ . My favorite image result was a collage of *Men's Health* magazine covers. Every single one of the cover boys were ripped with nice abs. I put it in my movie.

A few years later, the pandemic hit, and lockdowns happened.

An unexpected email popped in my inbox, stating that I had been nominated for *Best Self Magazine's Over 40 and Fabulous Contest*. I chuckled to myself because the previous cover winners were mostly beautiful, middle-aged White women, and here I am a young Black guy. But since I had extra time on my hands, I thought "Heck, why not?" and completed the form to enter the contest.

Over the coming weeks and months, I made the top forty finalists, then the top ten, then we had a photo shoot and interviews. And on the final day of the contest, the editor revealed the magazine cover. I couldn't believe it . . . it was me! My jaw dropped and tears streamed down my face. It was so surreal to see myself on the cover of an actual magazine, with thousands of copies distributed online and across the state.

I thought back to my Vision Movie™ . I didn't set out with the intention of being on a magazine cover, but the images I used for my fitness visualization all *happened to be* images of magazine covers. My subconscious decided this outcome for me, and it worked out the details with the universe.

What seems like serendipity or coincidence is often part of a grander scheme that is unfolding. To do your part, trust the process, notice these synchronicities, and take swift action when it's your time to do the work.

We will examine this in depth in the next chapter, where we will integrate your Vision Movie™ into your daily routine and empower your subconscious mind to attract the abundant life of your dreams.

KEY TAKEAWAYS

- Write a list of what you want to DO, BE, HAVE/KEEP, LEARN, CHANGE, and GIVE during this life.
- Find uplifting images that correspond with the experiences on your list.
- Use the images to create a moving slideshow, or Vision Movie™.
- Supplement your Vision Movie™ with vision boards and screensavers to immerse yourself in your new, soon-to-be reality.
- With repetition, your brain will feel the emotions and will begin to normalize this new reality. Then your subconscious will guide your decisions and actions to make your desired experiences real.

INSIGHTS

Use this space to write your reflections from this chapter.

What is one insight I learned about myself in regards to my life experiences?

_____

_____

_____

_____

_____

_____

_____

_____

_____

_____

What is my commitment to action?

_____

_____

_____

_____

_____

_____

_____

_____

_____

_____

CHAPTER 11:
INTEGRATING THE PRINCIPLES

"The times when I am running the best are when it feels effortless. The body is on autopilot, doing what you have trained it to do."
—Perdita Felicien, World Champion hurdler

OVERVIEW

We began this book with the metaphor of airplane wings in constant motion, continuously adjusting in anticipation of, or reaction to, external conditions. Did you also know that an airplane is on autopilot 90% of the time?[17]

World-famous pastor Joel Osteen says, "One study says that 90 percent of our everyday behavior is based on our habits. . . . That means how we treat people, how we spend our money, what we watch, what we listen to— 90 percent of the time, we're on autopilot. We do what we've always done."

The key to implementing the things you have learned in this book is to make them habitual and involuntary. Once you implement these habits into your daily life, they become ingrained into your subconscious, and you will be doing much of what we've learned in the preceding chapters on autopilot.

---

[17] John Cox, "Ask the Captain: How often is autopilot engaged?" *USA Today*, August 11, 2014, https://www.usatoday.com/story/travel/columnist/cox/2014/08/11/autopilot-control-takeoff-cruising-landing/13921511/

Think about that for a moment. Abundance in all areas of your life . . . on *autopilot!* But this will not happen overnight. The path to get there is through repetition and immersion.

STARTING YOUR DAY

I challenge you to follow the daily routine that I am about to explain below, for thirty continuous days. You can do anything for a short period of time, and thirty days gives you enough repetition to start seeing real results in your life.

If thirty days seems daunting to you, then consider this: I recently interviewed James Lawrence, also known as The Iron Cowboy. He holds the world record for the most Ironman-distance triathlons completed within a single calendar year.

The Iron Cowboy completed a full Ironman—that's a 2.4-mile swim (3.9K), a 112-mile bike ride (180.2K), and a 26.2-mile run (42.2K)—every single day for 101 consecutive days.

During our interview, he said something that stuck with me (I'm paraphrasing from memory): "If I can do this for 100 days straight, then you can do whatever you set your mind to for 100 days straight. Commit to doing something, *anything* positive, for 100 consecutive days, and see how your life changes."

I'm not asking you for 100 days, I'm only asking for thirty . . . but 100 would be even better. Committing to 365 days would be even better than that, but I want you to start small, so you can psychologically feel the win.

Every morning, first thing—have your Vision Movie™ playing in front of you, or in your peripheral vision, while you write your three

Gratitude statements, and your fifteen affirmations (see CHAPTER 5: SUBCONSCIOUS RESTRUCTURING).

Then meditate for ten to twenty minutes.

After that, go for a round of exercise—about thirty-five minutes of vigorous exercise—while listening to podcasts or an audiobook. If you can do this outside, even better, to get the benefits of fresh air and Vitamin D.

You may consider listening to material about an area in which you are experiencing a deficiency. A book about money or strengthening relationships, for example, if that applies to your current situation. This is how you combine multiple aspects of the SIMPLE framework into your everyday life so that you accomplish a lot in a small amount of time. Some suggested durations are below.

Now you have started your day with:

- Gratitude (5 minutes)
- Affirmations (10 minutes)
- Meditation (20 minutes)
- Exercise (35 minutes)
- Reading (10 minutes, and/or while you exercise)

This spells the acronym *GAMER*.

As a bonus, consider writing or publishing a video to *share* something you learned via social media or an article or your blog. Or maybe write it as a chapter to be later published in your book. Depending on the type of content, the act of writing can be cathartic or emotionally therapeutic. If it is educational content, writing about it or publishing videos will reinforce the learning, *and* you will be adding value to the world, which ultimately benefits you even more.

Famous entrepreneur, Gary Vaynerchuck says "Whether you like it or not, every person is now a media company . . . producing content is now the BASELINE for all brands and companies. It literally doesn't matter what business you're in, what industry you operate in, if you're not producing content, you basically don't exist."

So if you add in that last "S" for *Sharing*, which can take as little as ten minutes per day, you now have the acronym *GAMERS*.

For me, this is easy to remember because life can feel like we're in a massive multiplayer game, and we all have a finite amount of time in the game. So in essence, we are all GAMERS.

You may be thinking to yourself, "Who has ninety minutes to commit to this routine?" But I assure you that the effects of investing this ninety minutes every day, consistently, compounded over time, will eventually add ten times more time and value to your life because you will operate with that much more focus and clarity, making decisions that maximize and multiply your time. Ninety minutes may seem like a lot, but it's less than 10% of your waking hours, assuming a sixteen-hour day.

Now you are physically and mentally primed to go about your day. You will start to notice that things that used to annoy you don't bother you as much anymore. You will also feel more energized and in control of your day because you started with this strong foundation, and you are excited about the life you are designing.

DURING YOUR DAY

Every day, most of us are faced with the whirlwind of traffic, emails, text messages, notifications, phone calls, and meetings, plus the occasional really good news or really bad news that can send our emotions off the grid.

But now you are better prepared to face this whirlwind because, like a tall, structurally sound skyscraper, you took the time to build a strong foundation.

During your morning routine above, you covered the areas of:

S – Subconscious restructuring and spirituality, through the acts of gratitude journaling and meditation

I – Intellectual improvement, through listening to audiobooks and/ or reading and writing

M – Money – possibly, if your reading material was on the subject

P – Physical presence, through exercise

L – Love – but at this point in the day only self-love, by showing appreciation for what you have, which is vitally important

E – Entertaining experiences, by painting a picture of your future through visualization and written affirmations

Now, during your day, devote some time to your Money by going through your accounts and reviewing your expenses, your income streams, investments, and your net worth. Remember, that which you focus on expands. Even if you just spend five minutes looking at your online accounts, that is better than nothing.

Also, during your day, devote some time to nurturing relationships that you want to keep in the Continuance Phase. This could be as much or as little as a phone conversation during your commute, or a message to say "I was just thinking of you," or sending flowers or a handwritten card through an online service. Think of what that person's Love Language might be (see CHAPTER

9: LOVE & LEADERSHIP) and try to communicate with them in their language.

If you are managing people at the office, go around and speak to them. Show genuine interest in their personal lives (Leadership). It shouldn't feel rigid or systematic, though. There is a term called "management by wandering around" (MBWA) that was inspired by the Japanese *gemba walk* method developed at Toyota. The term means "the actual place" and refers to the act of managing by actually being physically present, which not only fosters relationships but also lends to leaner work execution and better quality control.

And of course, your time after work hours could be devoted to social, romantic, and/or family relationships, depending on your situation (Love). Or that time could be devoted to your side hustle (Money). Remember, it's all about evaluating your current levels in each area of your life day to day and calibrating accordingly.

ENDING YOUR DAY

At the end of your day, just before you go to sleep, write down three amazing things that happened that day for which you are thankful. It could be something as tiny as a moment of laughter from your child or the beautiful sunshine or the fact that you have full use of your fingers. Only focus on and write down the positive things.

Then meditate again for ten to twenty minutes before you drift off to sleep. If any to-do thoughts pop into your mind while you are meditating, jot them down to get them out of your head so that you can sleep peacefully.

FORMING BENEFICIAL ADDICTIONS

The key to winning with integrating the SIMPLE system is to get addicted to things that will help you level up in every area where you are deficient.

We have two motivators in life: pleasure and pain. Every action we take is ultimately to move us towards pleasure and away from pain.

With that said, here are some objections that may be ringing in your mind:

- What if I find meditation boring (pain)?
- What if I find exercise painful (pain)?
- What if reading is boring to me (pain)?
- What if I don't reach out in relationships because I'm scared of rejection (pain)?

These are all valid arguments that we as humans have probably all experienced. After all, if the majority of people found these things pleasurable, then we would all already be doing them and there would be no need for this book.

What I am going to teach you to do is to reverse-engineer the pain so that you find pleasure in each one of these things, and it would be painful for you to *not* do them on a regular basis.

I call this process forming beneficial addictions. We could say good habits, but for lasting transformation, I believe we must transcend habits. When you are addicted to something, there's no way you won't do it. You crave it. An intervention would be needed to make you stop.

Here's how you manufacture beneficial addictions:

Trigger the happy hormones (pleasure)

Meet the core human needs (pleasure)

Create disgust for the old behavior (pain)

Replicate post-traumatic growth (pain)

Get an accountability partner (both pleasure and pain)

TRIGGER THE HAPPY HORMONES

There are four major chemicals in our brain that influence our happiness:

Dopamine – think "dope" – Pleasurable experiences, as well as learning, memory, and motor system function, are all linked to dopamine. Dopamine is primarily related to the *anticipation* of a reward.[18] Like the excitement you feel when you're about to go on vacation or the thrill of rolling the dice in anticipation of the result.

Oxytocin – think "others" – Being around other people, including physical intimacy, such as kissing, hugging, and intercourse, raises oxytocin levels.[19]

Serotonin – think "sleep and sunshine" – Serotonin helps regulate your mood as well as your sleep, appetite, digestion, learning ability, and memory. They say people have a "sunny disposition" because sunshine

---

[18] Dr. Francisco Tigre Moura, "Dopamine: More Than Pleasure, The Secret is the Anticipation of a Reward," *LiveInnovation.org,* April 2, 2020, https://liveinnovation.org/dopamine-more-than-pleasure-the-secret-is-the-anticipation-of-a-reward/

[19] Maureen Salamon, "11 Interesting Effects of Oxytocin," *Live Science,* May 30, 2013, https://www.livescience.com/35219-11-effects-of-oxytocin.html

literally improves your mood by increasing serotonin and Vitamin D levels.[20]

Endorphins – think "exercise" – Endorphins are natural pain relievers produced by your body in reaction to stress or discomfort. Also, when you engage in reward-producing activities like eating, working out, or having sex, your endorphin levels tend to rise.[21]

When you do activities that release these hormones, you are more likely to get addicted to those activities.[22] This is why gambling, sex, and social media are so appealing and addictive. But there are ways to trigger the release of these chemicals in activities that you currently dislike. For example, I used to hate running. I had asthma. My knees hurt. It was painful.

Then I ran my first organized race, the Peachtree Road Race, which I described in CHAPTER 8: PHYSICAL PRESENCE. Ever heard of runner's high? It's literally a drug addiction to the happy, natural chemicals released in your brain.

Let's examine the science behind why this race was so transformative for me. Dopamine was released because I was excited with anticipation about conquering something new. Oxytocin was released because there were some 60,000 other humans in close proximity and the energy was high, like being at a concert. Serotonin was released because it was a beautiful, sunny day on the Fourth of July, one of the hottest days of the year in the USA. And endorphins were released because I was doing vigorous exercise, and endorphins are the body's natural pain reliever.

---

[20] Debbie Hampton, "The Relationship Between Sunshine, Serotonin, Vitamin D, and Depression," *The Best Brain Possible*, July 1, 2018, https://thebestbrainpossible.com/sunshine-vitamin-d-depression-serotonin/

[21] "Why Do We Need Endorphins?" *Healthline*, https://www.healthline.com/health/endorphins

[22] Kris Oyen, "RE 336: Endorphins, Dopamine, Serotonin, & Oxytocin," *Recovery Elevator*, July 26, 2021, https://www.recoveryelevator.com/re-336-endorphins-dopamine-serotonin-oxytocin/

So all four happy hormones were released in massive quantities, and I will never forget that high feeling. It was better than any drug I had ever tried. That was in 2008, and ever since then, I have participated in multiple races every year.

I went from dreading running to being addicted to it. Now it's rare that I ever go more than two days without running. Whenever that happens, I get cranky and irritable. It feels like I'm not quite myself. Running has become such an important part of my life—rebalancing, releasing happy hormones, and giving me clarity and focus—that I now find it hard to operate at my highest level without it.

Where can you orchestrate a situation in your life in which the happy hormones are released while you do something beneficial for you? Something that will move you closer to being the best version of yourself?

MEET THE CORE HUMAN NEEDS

According to Tony Robbins, there are six core human needs:

1. Certainty
2. Variety
3. Significance
4. Love/connection
5. Growth
6. Contribution

The first four needs shape our behavior and personality. The last two are spiritual needs.

A mentor once taught me that if three of the top four core needs are met by something, then we feel fulfilled by that thing.

Take marriage, for example. If your spouse gives you a feeling of reliability and security, that they will always be there for you no matter what, then your Certainty need is met.

If your spouse keeps things spontaneous, and full of good surprises, then your Variety need is met.

If your spouse frequently praises you and makes you feel important, then your Significance need is met.

And if your spouse expresses love for you—you spend time together and feel connected—then your Love/Connection need is met.

But what happens when two or more of those needs aren't met by your spouse? What if he/she takes you for granted, and you no longer feel Significant? What if they're never around, and you don't feel Certainty? What if things are the same, day in and day out, and you don't have Variety?

Because you're human, you'll be inclined to get those needs met somewhere else. And if three of the four needs are met elsewhere, then the relationship may be doomed.

So in each of the six SIMPLE dimensions of life, not just relationships, the key is to be aware of any areas where you don't feel fulfilled and take action to meet those needs in a beneficial way.

CREATE DISGUST FOR THE OLD BEHAVIOR

There are four phases of our connection with a behavior:

1. **Disgusted** – you hate it.
2. **Ambivalent** – you dabble, and might do it or not. No real connection to the behavior.

3. **Habitual** – you regularly do it.
4. **Addicted** – you can't stop doing it, even if it might be harmful.

You don't necessarily always go through these phases in step-by-step order. Depending on your experience, and the behavior, you could possibly skip from, say, ambivalence to addiction. And you might never be disgusted by some behaviors. It all depends.

If you're addicted to something, the only real way to break it is to become disgusted by it. You can remove it from your environment, but if you still yearn for it, then the addiction isn't broken.

So if you've tried going cold turkey, but that doesn't work, then how do you create disgust? Read on.

REPLICATE POST-TRAUMATIC GROWTH

We've all probably heard of post-traumatic stress disorder (PTSD). We usually hear about it with war veterans who suffered injuries, lost friends to battle, and witnessed horrible acts. But PTSD can affect civilians too. According to PTSD research, an estimated 75% of people will experience a traumatic event in their lifetime.[23]

Trauma can have lasting negative effects, including paranoia, depression, and suicide. But it can have positive effects too. According to a study from psychologists at the University of North Carolina, Charlotte, trauma changes people in fundamental ways, but surprisingly, the majority of the 600 trauma survivors they interviewed reported that their lives had changed for the better. Survivors of all types reported they had far more inner strength than they had

---

[23] Breslau, Naomi & Kessler, Ronald. (2001). "The stressor criterion in DSM-IV Posttraumatic Stress Disorder: An empirical investigation." *Biological psychiatry*. 50. 699-704. 10.1016/ S0006-3223(01)01167-2.

ever imagined, that they were closer to friends and family members, that life had more purpose, or that they were reorienting their lives toward more meaningful goals.

This phenomenon is referred to as *post-traumatic growth*—a term coined by two psychologists, Richard Tedeschi and Lawrence Calhoun, at the University of North Carolina in the 1980s[24]—or *post-traumatic greatness* (PTG), as my colleague Nic Haralambous puts it.

My carjacking was a traumatic experience. For more than a year after the incident, I remember being paranoid whenever I would enter or exit a vehicle. I would jump when a grocery cart clanged behind me in the grocery store parking lot.

But more importantly, I had decided that I was never going back to my old environment. This fear forced me to do something greater with my life, to seek a higher purpose. The key phrase here is "never going back." The traumatic experience elevated my baseline to a new level and forced me to pursue higher heights.

It's the same thing we see with fictional superheroes—they all have a traumatic origin story. Batman's parents were murdered right in front of him when he was a child. Superman's entire planet was destroyed, including his biological parents, and he grew up in a foreign land, trying to keep his identity secret. Our mythological heroes are the paragons of post-traumatic greatness. Art imitates life, and life imitates art.

So what if you haven't had a traumatic experience to elevate you in this manner? Count your blessings. Then pretend as if you did. Imagine in your mind what will happen if you continue down the same path, with the same detrimental behavior. Play the whole thing out in your mind

---

[24] Jim Rendon, "How Trauma Can Change You—For the Better," *Time*, July 22, 2015, https://time.com/3967885/how-trauma-can-change-you-for-the-better/

and imagine the *worst* that could happen. Feel the pain. Would you end up lonely? Sick? Publicly shamed? Homeless? Hospitalized? Dead?

Let your imagination fuel your disgust so that you never go back. And every time you feel your old desires coming back, ramp up your feeling of disgust again.

Here's an example of how I imagined trauma in my life: Back in 2012, I read a book called *Wheat Belly*. It described all of the damaging effects of processed wheat in modern-day society—belly fat, brain disease, decreased bone health, rapid aging, and even some cancers. After reading it, I challenged myself to try going without any wheat for three weeks. Not only did I lose weight, but I also felt mentally clearer. I imagined what I would look and feel like if I ever ate bread again, and the thought disgusted me. It still does. So much now that my body has developed a physical intolerance to wheat. Since then, when I have accidentally eaten wheat on occasion, I have paid the price with sharp stomach pains and ended up glued to the toilet all day with diarrhea and cold sweats. The thought disgusts me, and I'm never going back.

Where can you imagine trauma in your life so that you *never go back* to whatever behavior is keeping you from being your greatest self?

GET AN ACCOUNTABILITY PARTNER

It's hard to break old habits and form new habits alone. Willpower isn't enough.

Think about how you acquired the habit of brushing your teeth. More than likely a parent had to make you do it over and over again. Then after a few years, they only had to remind you occasionally. And now, you probably just do it on your own out of habit.

In the early stages of habit forming, we need someone to not only teach us how to do something, but then to yell at us and make us do it repeatedly until the new habit is ingrained in us to do it on our own.

When it came to my spiritual breakthrough with meditation, I paid $1,000 for a four-day immersive program led by a certified instructor.

When it came to my first physical breakthrough, my older brother trained with me and gave me the needed push. Then with my second physical breakthrough, I had a trainer to refine my steps and hold me accountable.

Before I got married, we went to premarital counseling. Twenty years later, we still refer to some of the materials and lessons learned.

I'm not perfect, so throughout the years, I've hired therapists to help me work through the tough spots in my personal and professional journeys.

In business, I've hired multiple coaches, enrolled in courses, joined peer groups and masterminds. Just this year alone, I've spent about $80,000 on various coaching and accountability programs.

My point is, don't try to do this on your own. Get expert support.

Many people are always looking for shortcuts. The real shortcut to success is expert support combined with accountability.

This combination can save you decades of trial and error. So build accountability into your life in those areas you want to enhance in a powerful way.

"Learn from the mistakes of others. You can't live long enough to make them all yourself.
—Eleanor Roosevelt

"It is important to learn from your mistakes, but it is better to learn from other people's mistakes, and it is best to learn from other people's successes. It accelerates your own success. "
—Jim Rohn

You could try to work with someone you know, like a friend or family member, but the danger there is that sometimes that person will project their own fears onto you. Or they simply lack the specific experience and expertise that you need.

If you are interested in working with me, or with someone on my team, to guide you to success in any area where you may need help, please reach out to me via my website, EthanKing.com

KEY TAKEAWAYS

- Begin each day with the GAMERS routine.
- End each day with gratitude and meditation.
- Form beneficial addictions, so that you are always doing what you love, and you can live an abundant life on autopilot.
- The shortcut to success is expert support combined with accountability.

CHAPTER 12:
DECISION-MAKING

"Sometimes it's the smallest decisions that can change your life forever."
—Keri Russell

"We are the sum total of the choices we have made."
—Eleanor Roosevelt

OVERVIEW

At its core, the SIMPLE system is a decision-making framework. Every decision we make, no matter how large or small it may seem, impacts the larger picture of our life.

Researchers at Cornell University estimated that the average adult makes around 35,000 choices per day. Some are major, and some are minor, but every single one of those choices impacts something else. What may seem like a small, insignificant choice may indirectly lead to a much bigger outcome, weeks or years down the road.

So when assessing your current levels in spirituality, intellect, physicality, money, love, and experiences, how do you decide what real-time calibrations to make? Ask key questions to help you prioritize and make decisions aligned with your goals, mission and vision.

KEY QUESTIONS

The first question to ask yourself is: "Can I put this off until a later date?"

You can't decide ten years from now to be present at your son's Little League games.

It's hard to make it up to your daughter if you miss her wedding.

The second question to ask yourself is: "Which thing, if I do it first, will make the rest of the things easier?"

For example, if you need to:

- Return business calls
- Hire an assistant
- Book an upcoming trip, and
- Schedule your house cleaning

Then it might make sense to do it in this order:

1. Take the next step in hiring an assistant—post the job, review candidates, conduct interviews—because eventually, your assistant can help you do things like the other three . . .
2. Return business calls
3. Book an upcoming trip
4. Schedule your house cleaning

The third question to ask yourself is: "What would the best, most evolved version of me do?"

With this exercise, you are going to create an imaginary advisor.

Imagine that in some parallel universe, there is a "perfect" version of you who made all of the right decisions and has it all. Or perhaps visualize an older, wiser version of you who is extremely well put together and knows exactly the right thing to say and do, in every situation.

Give this person a name, like *Ideal You* or *Elder You.*

In your mind's eye, go to that sage version of you, present the situation, and ask "What would you do?" More on this in the next chapter.

The fourth question to ask yourself is: "Can I take any action to affect this right now?"

Let me tell you a story.

Several years ago, I was in the business fight of my life.

An organization with whom we previously partnered served us with a frivolous lawsuit. It cost us months of nuisance, agony, and distraction, plus several hundred thousand dollars in lost revenue and legal fees.

I found out that several other companies were getting sued by these greedy thieves at the same time. Things got scary when we saw some of those other companies go bankrupt.

The situation felt very similar to that time when I was robbed at gunpoint, except this time I couldn't run. By the rules of tort law, we had to fight it or we'd risk losing everything. Fighting a lawsuit costs money, time, and stress, so either way I lose.

We hired the best attorneys around, but in between filing motions and trying to keep our business alive, there wasn't much else we could do. The situation was largely out of our control. It kept me up at night. I didn't know when this hell would end, but I needed a win.

So I decided to do something very unorthodox. In the middle of this mess, I started training for my first full marathon. If you've ever run a marathon, you know that the training leading up to it requires hours upon hours of long runs. Sometimes three to four hours of running per day, multiple days per week, for several months.

Some of my business peers thought I was crazy. They thought that instead of spending all that time training, I should have been working to save my business instead. But I persisted and I finished the marathon.

With the struggles I was going through, crossing that finish line after 26.2 miles gave me a tremendous sense of personal accomplishment. Finishing that race was the victory I needed. Though it may have been completely unrelated to what was going on in my business, it was still a win.

A few months later, we countersued the other party, and the case was settled outside of court.

At the time, I didn't know it, but the changes that we were forced to make to our business during that time catapulted us to a higher level once the lawsuit settled. Thus, in the end, even the lawsuit turned out to be truly good for us.

My point is that sometimes you've done all you can do in one area, so leave that in God's hands and keep winning in the other areas. Don't let those other areas get pulled down too. The beauty of this model is that focusing on the other areas can sometimes pull the deficient area up too. The obvious approach isn't always the best approach for every situation.

KEY TAKEAWAYS

- Ask the key questions to decide which actions to take right now.
- Accept that sometimes things will be out of your control.
- Sometimes the obvious answer isn't the best answer.
- Focus on what you can control, and the rest will work itself out.

CHAPTER 13: FINAL THOUGHTS

"Become who you might become, instead of staying who you are."
—*Jordan Peterson*

Albert Einstein concluded that past, present, and future exist simultaneously, and that time is an illusion. Some quantum physicists believe that parallel universes, or multiple dimensions, exist. I believe there are an infinite number of dimensions, each a different version because of the compound decisions and actions that we have all made and the ripple effect of each choice. In many of these dimensions, there exist better versions of me. In one of these dimensions exists the *best* version of me. I strive to shape my world into his world and become him.

Imagine for a moment that another version of you walked through the door right now. Same age, same exact DNA, but this version of you is everything you want to be—cooler, smarter, healthier, better looking, better love life, richer, more polished, more ambitious, more successful—all because he or she made different choices in life. How would it make you feel to come face to face with that person?

Someone once told me that hell on Earth would be if, on your dying day, you were to meet the person you *could* have become. That thought makes me shiver. It is what motivates me.

I want to be the best possible version of myself. I don't want to meet the man I *could* have become and feel anguish because I didn't realize my full potential.

So when faced with a decision, I ask myself, "What would the best, most evolved version of Ethan do?" It is as if that uber-version of me is my imaginary advisor. Don't get me wrong, I am far from perfect. I often make terrible decisions and fall short of the mark. But I do try to put every choice through this filter.

Since I'm constantly trying to train my brain to think this way, I once tried sticking a note to my bathroom mirror that says, "What would the best, most evolved version of Ethan do?" But the note fell off, and I forgot about it.

Then I figured, since I own a clothing company, why not make myself a t-shirt?

Inspired by the genius inventor and Renaissance artist Leonardo da Vinci, who was known to write his thoughts in mirror script, I designed a t-shirt using his same mirror script. Unlike most t-shirts, this shirt wasn't designed for others to read. It's illegible when others read it. You can only read it when looking in a mirror. It was designed for me, to remind myself of the choices I need to make to continuously level up in life.

Now when I look in the mirror, the question is repeatedly driven into my subconscious, rewiring my neurons always to think in this way. I believe that this life hack empowers me to make smarter decisions that move me closer to where I want to be, faster.

I even sleep in this shirt so that whenever I wake up and look in the bathroom mirror, my subconscious is reminded.

If you'd like to try this concept for yourself, I invite you to get your own EVOLVE shirt: **EvolveShirt.com**

Wear it for a year. Wear it often. Sleep in it. Then, twelve months from now, let me know how your life was impacted. If nothing changed, you can return it.

Use tools like this shirt and the other resources at *SIMPLE Success School* to guide your choices so that you may go forth and become the best possible version of *you.*

The frameworks I have described in this book are the authentic tools I use to govern my life. They work for me, they work for others, and will work for you too. You are now equipped to do the work, follow the steps, and design the life of your dreams. I believe in you and look forward to one day hearing about your journey to a full life.

Please find my social media handles at www.EthanKing.com and send me a message to let me know how this book has impacted you. Share with me some of your "Aha!" moments as you implement the changes in your life and see the magic unfold. I hope to one day meet you in person at an event, where you can tell me firsthand how things have changed for the better.

Remember, you can have it all.

ETHAN KING

ABOUT THE AUTHOR

Ethan King is an American entrepreneur, a passionate experiential learner, and thought leader in life & style optimization.

He owns multiple businesses in apparel, e-commerce, fitness, and real estate.

He is cofounder of *stuff4GREEKS*—an industry leading provider of custom fraternity and sorority gear.

He is cofounder of *Zeus' Closet*—a network of retail and e-commerce brands dedicated to personalized apparel. It's like a tattoo shop for your clothes®.

Through his keynote talks and programs, Ethan shares actionable lessons learned along his journey from starving artist to CEO of multiple 7-figure businesses.

On the personal front, Ethan overcame struggles with asthma and obesity to transform his physical appearance, which eventually landed him on the cover of *Best Self Magazine*. This inspired him to help other middle-aged peers achieve their fitness goals through his *6-pack Mindset* programs, including *6-pack Moms* and *6-pack Dads*.

Ethan coaches high-performing entrepreneurs and professionals in various industries throughout the world, on science-based methods to help design the life they really desire. He believes you can truly have it all, in every dimension of life, without sacrificing what matters.

Ethan currently resides in Atlanta, Georgia, with his wife, Monica, and their two children, Imana and Legend.

RESOURCES

SIMPLE SUCCESS SCHOOL

To find any of the programs mentioned in this book, visit **www.simplesuccess.school**

- *The Wealth Beyond Money Companion Journal*
- *Get in Game: Gratitude, Affirmation, Meditation Exercises*
- *Start → Become Your Own Boss program*
- *Scale → Roadmap To Your First Million program*
- *Systematize → How To Run A $1m/Year+ Business*
- *The Double Your Revenue Dashboard*
- *From Drowning In Debt to Debt-Free Masterclass*
- *And more*

SIMPLE Success School is a growing library of books, courses, and training programs to help you prosper in each of life's 6 dimensions—Spirituality, Intellect, Money, Physicality, Love/Leadership, and Experiences.

ETHANKING.COM

This is the online hub for all things Ethan King.

Follow Ethan's blog, find links to connect with him on social media, and keep up with new programs and developments as they are released.

Please direct all booking inquires for speaking engagements to **https://EthanKing.com/**

6-PACK MINDSET

6-pack Mindset is a comprehensive transformation program for your body, built on 5 core pillars—mindset, science, fitness, nutrition, and accountability. Our flagship programs are *6-pack Moms* and *6-pack Dads*. We'll help you get 6-pack abs, in potentially as little as 6 weeks, without going to the gym or completely giving up the foods your love.

Ask about our weight loss guarantee programs. Learn more at **https://www.6packmindset.com/**

EVOLVESHIRT.COM

Get your own, personalized *Evolve T-Shirt,* as described in CHAPTER 13: FINAL THOUGHTS to level up your subconscious. Just go to **https://evolveshirt.com/**

REVIEWS

"In *Wealth Beyond Money,* Ethan King brings forward some of the most important aspects for business leaders and entrepreneurs in a straightforward, easy-to-read and understandable book. I was thrilled to see his '20 things that actually help me sleep' section, since he and I share knowledge of the importance of sleep. And I plan to use several of the personal finance tips…they were awesome!"

— Dr. Michael Breus, PhD aka the Sleep Doctor

www.thesleepdoctor.com

"*Wealth Beyond Money* is a cross between a juicy memoir and a highlight reel for cracking the code on life. This book is actionable. It covers nearly every category in life that brings meaning, heart, and purpose.

Ethan King teaches us to dream big and envision what we desire most. He gives us the tools to open our minds, grow, create change, and construct a holistic life. His idea of having it all could be true; after all, he is living proof.

I have wholeheartedly consumed this information, taking notes and taking action. What a gift this concise guide for life has been for me and possibly for you too."

—Darcie Adler, Founder/Creative Director

The Spin Style Agency LLC

thespinstyle.com

"Move over Tony Robbins, Ethan King's *Wealth Beyond Money* is the complete life guide to success. With the author's out-of-the-box concepts like 'AND instead of either' and 'Eliminate the lukewarm,' Ethan King rejects the 'balanced life' approach to living and advocates winning in all areas. Easy to understand, you will start applying his methods after just one chapter. I highly recommend this book for the next level in self-improvement and living to the fullest in every aspect of your life."
 —Maureen Ryan-Blake, Best Selling Author, TV Show Host, Publisher
 Founder of The Power of the Tribe Network
 https://thepowerofthetribe.com/

"If you 'want it all,' read this book! Ethan uses his own life experience to show you how. The story and experience with UGA President Michael Adams was priceless! The book is chock full of exercises and pathways you can use to make your road to financial success shorter and easier. You will find his Vision Matrix to be a handy tool.
Ethan's command of the English language is impressive, and his choice of words sticks with you. My personal favorite is how to be your "greatest self!' What a great book!"
 —Vincent M. Roazzi, President of Namaste Publications
 Author of the best-selling book, *The Spirituality of Success, Getting Rich with Integrity*
 Grand Prize Winner and Author of the Year in the New York DIY Book Festival
 Award-winning translation into 27 languages
 http://www.spiritualityofsuccess.com

"Take a pause and dive into this book. With a refreshing practical perspective and relatable examples, Ethan's book feels distinctly *real*. It's not theory or concepts. He takes you on a journey of raw life examples leading to the proven SIMPLE wisdom and daily habits accelerating his success today. And the integrated accountability exercises make implementation achievable. Probably most importantly, he left me thinking – 'What would the best, most evolved version of Brad do?'

As Ethan references, 'Hell on earth is meeting the person you could have become on your last day.' This book is a strong reminder I don't want to meet that person!"

 — Brad Stevens, Founder/CEO, OutsourceAccess.com
 https://www.facebook.com/bstevens44
 https://www.linkedin.com/in/bradstevens44/

"A powerfully simple approach to whole life success. King's book is a pocket compass. Use it to activate your inner guidance to be a better person, make the right decisions and live your best life."

 — Tanya Chernova, Award Winning Speaker, Tanya Chernova Global Corp
 Co-Founder Courageous Living
 @thetanyachernova
 www.tanyachernova.com

"Ethan's writing style kept me glued to the pages as I learned all about his entrepreneurial journey. There are so many tips, tricks and lessons learned throughout his journey that I consider this a must-read for all entrepreneurs, whether you are just starting or have been a lifetime entrepreneur like myself."

 — Steve Distante, CEO Vanderbilt Financial Group
 Entrepreneur, Founder, Chairman, Filmmaker, Farmer, Author and Investment Banker
 www.stevedistante.com

"Mindset and attitude are so important, and Ethan shares practical, proven wisdom about how to get your mind in a good place. I love the foundational principles and how Ethan finds ways of implementing them in his life, and in the lives of those that he leads. He is open and honest about his own life journey, and how it has not been an easy path. I find this book a positive inspiration for me."

— Conor Neill, President of Vistage in Spain & Professor at IESE Business School

www.conorneill.com, www.linkedin.com/in/conor

"For those looking to implement an intentional plan for their life, *Wealth Beyond Money* is a must read. Ethan King shares his personal experiences on the process he followed to transform his life from an aimless debt-ridden, unhealthy, single petty-thief to a successful, wealthy, picture-of-health, happily-married ROCK STAR. Ethan shares his actions and the deliverables he used to see his dreams become reality. *Wealth Beyond Money* is an enjoyable read that you will want to read to the end and then go back and re-read as you implement Ethan's proven plan to a healthy, happy, and fulfilled life."

— John Marshall, ReEngager, Community Builder, and Connection Maker

https://www.reengagenow.com

https://www.hlpster.com/st/johnmarshall

https://www.linkedin.com/in/johnmarshall4

"*Wealth Beyond Money* is a timely narrative, given society's movement towards greater spiritual and emotional fulfillment. The SIMPLE framework serves as a catalyst to reconfigure our minds on how we think about happiness, and Ethan King's life story is both entertaining and educational. A true must read."

— Samir Damani, MD, PharmD

Founder, CEO

iThriveMD

"Living a happy and fulfilled life is everyone's goal, and perhaps the most elusive goal. In this book, Ethan delivers direct access to that kind of life. Readers discover their capacity to continually re-invent themselves and live as someone who can create and sustain an integrated life, where sacrifices and suffering are assigned new meaning. *Wealth Beyond Money* is the ultimate collection of practices that anyone, at any time, can use to build generational wealth, live long healthy lives, create real intimacy in relationships, and lead themselves and others to make a lasting impact in life and in business."

— Saurel Quettan
Executive and Leadership Coach
ExeQfit, Inc.
https://exeqfit.com/
https://www.linkedin.com/in/saurelquettan/
https://www.facebook.com/saurelquettan

"Do you want an optimized life, finding fulfillment and success as you build your business? I find Ethan's perspective and methods invaluable as I seek my own! Without scouring the internet, now I have an action-packed resource to help me create an abundant, well-rounded life, business and legacy."

— Cody James Aikin, Host of the Pillars of Freedom Podcast
https://www.pillarsoffreedom.com/cody

"Ethan King does a masterful job explaining the constraints of balance with both personal and professional experiences. The SIMPLE framework makes the elusive work-life balance attainable for any kind of professional. *Wealth Beyond Money* is a collection of wise quotables based on business experiences and faith—an enjoyable read with a welcomed perspective. The chapter on Money Mastery helped me understand wealth as a ratio and not a dollar amount. Overall, this book helped me re-align with my purpose and put perspective to the pursuit of success."

— Dr. Ivan Salaberrios, President and Founder AIM Technical Services
https://www.aimtechnical.com
Twitter: @IvanSalaberrios

"What a refreshing and pragmatic read. I love practical, action-orientated messages, and I got just that.

Ethan managed to create a little life book with loads of tips and tricks for the reader.

It is great to have a handbook for many spheres in life and learn from someone else's experiences. Not only does this provide you with practical tips, but it also inspires and motivates you through the journey of Ethan's life, learning how he overcame obstacles when most people would have given up. Truly inspiring, and a good reminder that we have the ability to make things happen, to change our life script, and create a new story for the life we want."

— Heléne Smuts, Founder Credo Growth
LI: helenesmuts
FB, Insta: @helenetalks
www.credogrowth.com

"Rather than giving us advice on how to run our lives, Ethan shares experiences from his personal and professional life. Truly this book is a powerful tool that gets one thinking about applying these valuable lessons to one's own scenarios. Unlike what most of us think, Ethan shares an interesting fact–that we all have 6 packs, we just do not realize that we do. They are already inside of us! Ethan shows us ways to uncover the excess fat we have, be it limited mindset, useless efforts, or dormant qualities. Indeed a must read!"

— Abeer Qumsieh, Founder and CEO Better Business
@Abeerqumsieh

"The single biggest factor in determining success for an entrepreneur or investor are the 'mental models' we base our lives and effort around. With the right model, years of wasted effort (or money) can be avoided. Ethan's well-written book highlights the most important mental constructs that will serve you extremely well, not just in business but in life overall."

— Samir Patel
Managing Partner, Trophy Point High Yield Income
www.TrophyPointCapital.com

"This book is a must read! Through his story, Ethan not only educates, but also motivates. Even after just the first night of reading, I started applying the best practices to my everyday life.

My favorite chapter was Money Mastery, where Ethan discusses the meaning of true financial wealth. I immediately used the concepts to show my wife how to calculate our wealth score.

I participated in the 6-pack Dads program last year, and after reading this book I see why it worked so well for me. I lost over 30lbs by following the steps Ethan shared. This book not only explains the trial and error of his success, but the science and research behind why we do what we do.

I will definitely be reading this book again to take a deeper dive on *all* components. This is a must-read, not only for up-and-coming entrepreneurs, but for anyone who wants something different in life, whether it is to make more money, live a healthy lifestyle, or just have better relationship with your spouse or friends."

— Kris Favers, Marketing Professional

"The fundamentals to success in life are not a mystery. They are a series of actions and habits that add up over time. Ethan King makes this journey SIMPLE for you. Ethan isn't preaching from the mountain tops about what you should do, he is sharing his experience. It is clear he walks the walk and talks the talk. The fundamentals outlined in this book are a great reality check and have helped me assess where I've been, where I'm at, and where I want to go. Thank you, Ethan, for sharing your story, your experience, and your expertise and for challenging me to live a life focused on greater wealth, health, and happiness."

— Dr. Justin Scott, Founder
Pure Dental Health
IG: @puredentalhealth

"I have had many great conversations with Ethan King about life and business. His new book, *Wealth Beyond Money*, is a fantastic summary of many of our conversations and so much more. It is a great source for anyone wanting to 'figure it out' and/or get a little 'tune up' on what they already know. While reading it, I said to myself several times, 'Yeah, I need to do that!'... 'And that!'... 'And oh of course, I need to get back to doing that, too.'

I highly suggest reading *Wealth Beyond Money* so you too can have some actionable steps to help you on your journey of a successful & fulfilled life."

— Marshall Chiles, Serial Entrepreneur

https://www.linkedin.com/in/marshallchiles/

"This book is full of actionable tips that are easy to understand, and the stories helped me navigate through a very challenging time with my family's health. The concept of 'SIMPLE' really resonates with me. I am thankful for the wisdom Ethan King shares in *Wealth Beyond Money*, and I believe every person who desires well-rounded success should have this book in her library."

— Smita

Indie pop star, TV Host, Entrepreneur, Social Activist

@smitapop

Made in the USA
Columbia, SC
12 April 2023

378a9db3-c942-458d-a138-15dd85881ef5R01

CONTENTS

Book One

1 EVERY ART AND every inquiry, and similarly every action and pursuit, is thought to aim at some good; and for this reason the good has rightly been declared to be that at which all things aim. But a certain difference is found among ends; some are activities, others are products apart from the activities that produce them. Where there are ends apart from the actions, it is the nature of the products to be better than the activities. Now, as there are many actions, arts, and sciences, their ends also are many; the end of the medical art is health, that of shipbuilding a vessel, that of strategy victory, that of economics wealth. But where such arts fall under a single capacity – as bridle-making and the other arts concerned with the equipment of horses fall under the art of riding, and this and every military action under strategy, in the same way other arts fall under yet others – in all of these the ends of the master arts are to be preferred to all the subordinate ends; for it is for the sake of the former that the latter are pursued. It makes no difference whether the activities themselves are the ends of the actions, or something else apart from the activities, as in the case of the sciences just mentioned.

2 If, then, there is some end of the things we do, which we desire for its own sake (everything else being desired for the sake of this), and if we do not choose everything for the sake of something else (for at that rate the process would go on to infinity, so that our desire would be empty and vain), clearly this must be the good and the chief good. Will not the knowledge of it, then, have a great influence on life? Shall we not, like archers who have a mark to aim at, be more likely to hit upon what is right? If so, we must try, in outline at least, to determine what it is, and of which of the sciences or capacities it is the object. It would seem to belong to the most authoritative art and that which is most truly the master art. And politics appears to be of this nature; for it is this that ordains which of the sciences should

be studied in a state, and which each class of citizens should learn and up to what point they should learn them; and we see even the most highly esteemed of capacities to fall under this, e.g. strategy, economics, rhetoric; now, since politics uses the rest of the sciences, and since, again, it legislates as to what we are to do and what we are to abstain from, the end of this science must include those of the others, so that this end must be the good for man. For even if the end is the same for a single man and for a state, that of the state seems at all events something greater and more complete whether to attain or to preserve; though it is worth while to attain the end merely for one man, it is finer and more godlike to attain it for a nation or for city-states. These, then, are the ends at which our inquiry aims, since it is political science, in one sense of that term.

3 Our discussion will be adequate if it has as much clearness as the subject-matter admits of, for precision is not to be sought for alike in all discussions, any more than in all the products of the crafts. Now fine and just actions, which political science investigates, admit of much variety and fluctuation of opinion, so that they may be thought to exist only by convention, and not by nature. And goods also give rise to a similar fluctuation because they bring harm to many people; for before now men have been undone by reason of their wealth, and others by reason of their courage. We must be content, then, in speaking of such subjects and with such premises to indicate the truth roughly and in outline, and in speaking about things which are only for the most part true and with premises of the same kind to reach conclusions that are no better. In the same spirit, therefore, should each type of statement be received; for it is the mark of an educated man to look for precision in each class of things just so far as the nature of the subject admits; it is evidently equally foolish to accept probable reasoning from a mathematician and to demand from a rhetorician scientific proofs.

Now each man judges well the things he knows, and of these he is a good judge. And so the man who has been educated in a subject is a good judge of that subject, and the man who has received an all-round education is a good judge in general. Hence a young man is not a proper hearer of lectures on political science; for he is inexperienced in the actions that occur in life, but its discussions start from these and are about these; and, further, since he tends to follow his passions, his study will be vain and unprofitable, because the end aimed at is not knowledge but action. And it makes no difference whether he is young in years or youthful in character; the defect does not depend on time, but on his living, and pursuing each successive object, as passion directs. For to such persons, as to the incontinent, knowledge brings no profit; but to those who desire and act in accordance with a rational principle knowledge about such matters will be of great benefit.

These remarks about the student, the sort of treatment to be expected, and the purpose of the inquiry, may be taken as our preface.

4 Let us resume our inquiry and state, in view of the fact that all knowledge and every pursuit aims at some good, what it is that we say political science aims at and what is the highest of all goods achievable by action. Verbally there is very general agreement; for both the general run of men and people of superior refinement say that it is happiness, and identify living well and doing well with being happy; but with regard to what happiness is they differ, and the many do not give the same account as the wise. For the former think it is some plain and obvious thing, like pleasure, wealth, or honour; they differ, however, from one another – and often even the same man identifies it with different things, with health when he is ill, with wealth when he is poor; but, conscious of their ignorance, they admire those who proclaim some great ideal that is above their comprehension. Now some thought that apart from these many goods there is another which is self-subsistent and causes the goodness of all these as well. To examine all the opinions that have been held were perhaps somewhat fruitless; enough to examine those that are most prevalent or that seem to be arguable.

Let us not fail to notice, however, that there is a difference between arguments from and those to the first principles. For Plato, too, was right in raising this question and asking, as he used to do, 'are we on the way from or to the first principles?' There is a difference, as there is in a race-course between the course from the judges to the turning-point and the way back. For, while we must begin with what is known, things are objects of knowledge in two sensessome to us, some without qualification. Presumably, then, we must begin with things known to us. Hence any one who is to listen intelligently to lectures about what is noble and just, and generally, about the subjects of political science must have been brought up in good habits. For the fact is the starting-point, and if this is sufficiently plain to him, he will not at the start need the reason as well; and the man who has been well brought up has or can easily get starting-points. And as for him who neither has nor can get them, let him hear the words of Hesiod:

Far best is he who knows all things himself;
Good, he that hearkens when men counsel right;
But he who neither knows, nor lays to heart
Another's wisdom, is a useless wight.

5 Let us, however, resume our discussion from the point at which we digressed. To judge from the lives that men lead, most men, and men of the most vulgar type, seem (not without some ground) to identify the good, or happiness, with pleasure; which is the reason why they love the life of enjoyment. For there are, we may say, three prominent types of life – that just mentioned, the political, and thirdly the contemplative life. Now the mass of mankind are evidently quite slavish in their tastes, preferring a life suitable to beasts, but they get some ground for their view from the fact that many of those in high places share the tastes of Sardanapallus. A consideration of the prominent types of life shows that people of superior refinement and of active disposition identify happiness with honour; for this is, roughly speaking, the end of the political life. But it seems too superficial to be what we are looking for, since it is thought to depend on those who bestow honour rather than on him who receives it, but the good we divine to be something proper to a man and not easily taken from him. Further, men seem to pursue honour in order that they may be assured of their goodness; at least it is by men of practical wisdom that they seek to be honoured, and among those who know them, and on the ground of their virtue; clearly, then, according to them, at any rate, virtue is better. And perhaps one might even suppose this to be, rather than honour, the end of the political life. But even this appears somewhat incomplete; for possession of virtue seems actually compatible with being asleep, or with lifelong inactivity, and, further, with the greatest sufferings and misfortunes; but a man who was living so no one would call happy, unless he were maintaining a thesis at all costs. But enough of this; for the subject has been sufficiently treated even in the current discussions. Third comes the contemplative life, which we shall consider later.

The life of money-making is one undertaken under compulsion, and wealth is evidently not the good we are seeking; for it is merely useful and for the sake of something else. And so one might rather take the afore-named objects to be ends; for they are loved for themselves. But it is evident that not even these are ends; yet many arguments have been thrown away in support of them. Let us leave this subject, then.

6 We had perhaps better consider the universal good and discuss thoroughly what is meant by it, although such an inquiry is made an

uphill one by the fact that the Forms have been introduced by friends of our own. Yet it would perhaps be thought to be better, indeed to be our duty, for the sake of maintaining the truth even to destroy what touches us closely, especially as we are philosophers or lovers of wisdom; for, while both are dear, piety requires us to honour truth above our friends.

The men who introduced this doctrine did not posit Ideas of classes within which they recognized priority and posteriority (which is the reason why they did not maintain the existence of an Idea embracing all numbers); but the term 'good' is used both in the category of substance and in that of quality and in that of relation, and that which is per se, i.e. substance, is prior in nature to the relative (for the latter is like an off shoot and accident of being); so that there could not be a common Idea set over all these goods. Further, since 'good' has as many senses as 'being' (for it is predicated both in the category of substance, as of God and of reason, and in quality, i.e. of the virtues, and in quantity, i.e. of that which is moderate, and in relation, i.e. of the useful, and in time, i.e. of the right opportunity, and in place, i.e. of the right locality and the like), clearly it cannot be something universally present in all cases and single; for then it could not have been predicated in all the categories but in one only. Further, since of the things answering to one Idea there is one science, there would have been one science of all the goods; but as it is there are many sciences even of the things that fall under one category, e.g. of opportunity, for opportunity in war is studied by strategics and in disease by medicine, and the moderate in food is studied by medicine and in exercise by the science of gymnastics. And one might ask the question, what in the world they mean by 'a thing itself', is (as is the case) in 'man himself' and in a particular man the account of man is one and the same. For in so far as they are man, they will in no respect differ; and if this is so, neither will 'good itself' and particular goods, in so far as they are good. But again it will not be good any the more for being eternal, since that which lasts long is no whiter than that which perishes in a day. The Pythagoreans seem to give a more plausible account of the good, when they place the one in the column of goods; and it is they that Speusippus seems to have followed.

But let us discuss these matters elsewhere; an objection to what we have said, however, may be discerned in the fact that the Platonists have not been speaking about all goods, and that the goods that are pursued and loved for themselves are called good by reference to a single Form, while those which tend to produce or to preserve these somehow or to prevent their contraries are called so by reference to these, and in a secondary sense. Clearly, then, goods must be spoken of in two ways, and some must be good in themselves, the others by reason of these. Let us separate, then, things good in themselves from things useful, and consider whether the former are called good by reference to a single Idea. What sort of goods would one call good in themselves? Is it those that are pursued even when isolated from others, such as intelligence, sight, and certain pleasures and honours? Certainly, if we pursue these also for the sake of something else, yet one would place them among things good in themselves. Or is nothing other than the Idea of good good in itself? In that case the Form will be empty. But if the things we have named are also things good in themselves, the account of the good will have to appear as something identical in them all, as that of whiteness is identical in snow and in white lead. But of honour, wisdom, and pleasure, just in respect of their goodness, the accounts are distinct and diverse. The good, therefore, is not some common element answering to one Idea.

But what then do we mean by the good? It is surely not like the things that only chance to have the same name. Are goods one, then, by being derived from one good or by all contributing to one good, or are they rather one by analogy? Certainly as sight is in the body, so is reason in the soul, and so on in other cases. But perhaps these subjects had better be dismissed for the present; for perfect precision about them would be more appropriate to another branch of philosophy. And similarly with regard to the Idea; even if there is some one good which is universally predicable of goods or is capable of separate and independent existence, clearly it could not be achieved or attained by man; but we are now seeking something attainable. Perhaps, however, some one might think it worth while to recognize this with a view to the goods that are attainable and achievable; for having this as a sort of pattern we shall know better the goods that are good for us, and if we know them shall attain them. This argument has some plausibility, but seems to clash with the procedure of the sciences; for all of these, though they aim at some good and seek to supply the deficiency of it, leave on one side the knowledge of the good. Yet that all the exponents of the arts should be ignorant of, and should not even seek, so great an aid is not probable. It is hard, too, to see how a weaver or a carpenter will be benefited in regard to his own craft by knowing this 'good itself', or how the man who has viewed the Idea itself will be a better doctor or general thereby. For a doctor seems not even to study health in this way, but the health of man, or perhaps

rather the health of a particular man; it is individuals that he is heal-
ing. But enough of these topics.

7 Let us again return to the good we are seeking, and ask what it
can be. It seems different in different actions and arts; it is different in
medicine, in strategy, and in the other arts likewise. What then is the
good of each? Surely that for whose sake everything else is done. In
medicine this is health, in strategy victory, in architecture a house, in
any other sphere something else, and in every action and pursuit the
end; for it is for the sake of this that all men do whatever else they do.
Therefore, if there is an end for all that we do, this will be the good
achievable by action, and if there are more than one, these will be the
goods achievable by action.

So the argument has by a different course reached the same point;
but we must try to state this even more clearly. Since there are evidently more than one end, and we choose some of these (e.g. wealth,
flutes, and in general instruments) for the sake of something else,
clearly not all ends are final ends; but the chief good is evidently
something final. Therefore, if there is only one final end, this will be
what we are seeking, and if there are more than one, the most final of
these will be what we are seeking. Now we call that which is in itself
worthy of pursuit more final than that which is worthy of pursuit for
the sake of something else, and that which is never desirable for the
sake of something else more final than the things that are desirable
both in themselves and for the sake of that other thing, and therefore
we call final without qualification that which is always desirable in
itself and never for the sake of something else.

Now such a thing happiness, above all else, is held to be; for this
we choose always for self and never for the sake of something else,
but honour, pleasure, reason, and every virtue we choose indeed for
themselves (for if nothing resulted from them we should still choose
each of them), but we choose them also for the sake of happiness,
judging that by means of them we shall be happy. Happiness, on the
other hand, no one chooses for the sake of these, nor, in general, for
anything other than itself.

From the point of view of self-sufficiency the same result seems to
follow; for the final good is thought to be self-sufficient. Now by self-
sufficient we do not mean that which is sufficient for a man by himself,
for one who lives a solitary life, but also for parents, children, wife, and in
general for his friends and fellow citizens, since man is born for citizen-
ship. But some limit must be set to this; for if we extend our requirement
to ancestors and descendants and friends' friends we are in for an infinite

series. Let us examine this question, however, on another occasion; the self-sufficient we now define as that which when isolated makes life desirable and lacking in nothing; and such we think happiness to be; and further we think it most desirable of all things, without being counted as one good thing among others – if it were so counted it would clearly be made more desirable by the addition of even the least of goods; for that which is added becomes an excess of goods, and of goods the greater is always more desirable. Happiness, then, is something final and self-sufficient, and is the end of action.

Presumably, however, to say that happiness is the chief good seems a platitude, and a clearer account of what it is still desired. This might perhaps be given, if we could first ascertain the function of man. For just as for a flute-player, a sculptor, or an artist, and, in general, for all things that have a function or activity, the good and the 'well' is thought to reside in the function, so would it seem to be for man, if he has a function. Have the carpenter, then, and the tanner certain functions or activities, and has man none? Is he born without a function? Or as eye, hand, foot, and in general each of the parts evidently has a function, may one lay it down that man similarly has a function apart from all these? What then can this be? Life seems to be common even to plants, but we are seeking what is peculiar to man. Let us exclude, therefore, the life of nutrition and growth. Next there would be a life of perception, but it also seems to be common even to the horse, the ox, and every animal. There remains, then, an active life of the element that has a rational principle; of this, one part has such a principle in the sense of being obedient to one, the other in the sense of possessing one and exercising thought. And, as 'life of the rational element' also has two meanings, we must state that life in the sense of activity is what we mean; for this seems to be the more proper sense of the term. Now if the function of man is an activity of soul which follows or implies a rational principle, and if we say 'so-and-so-and 'a good so-and-so' have a function which is the same in kind, e.g. a lyre, and a good lyre-player, and so without qualification in all cases, eminence in respect of goodness being idded to the name of the function (for the function of a lyre-player is to play the lyre, and that of a good lyre-player is to do so well): if this is the case, and we state the function of man to be a certain kind of life, and this to be an activity or actions of the soul implying a rational principle, and the function of a good man to be the good and noble performance of these, and if any action is well performed when it is performed in accordance with the appropriate excellence: if this is the case, human good turns out to be activity of soul in accordance with virtue, and if there are more than one virtue, in accordance with the best and most complete.

But we must add 'in a complete life.' For one swallow does not make a summer, nor does one day; and so too one day, or a short time, does not make a man blessed and happy.

Let this serve as an outline of the good; for we must presumably first sketch it roughly, and then later fill in the details. But it would seem that any one is capable of carrying on and articulating what has once been well outlined, and that time is a good discoverer or partner in such a work; to which facts the advances of the arts are due; for any one can add what is lacking. And we must also remember what has been said before, and not look for precision in all things alike, but in each class of things such precision as accords with the subject-matter, and so much as is appropriate to the inquiry. For a carpenter and a geometer investigate the right angle in different ways; the former does so in so far as the right angle is useful for his work, while the latter inquires what it is or what sort of thing it is; for he is a spectator of the truth. We must act in the same way, then, in all other matters as well, that our main task may not be subordinated to minor questions. Nor must we demand the cause in all matters alike; it is enough in some cases that the fact be well established, as in the case of the first principles; the fact is the primary thing or first principle. Now of first principles we see some by induction, some by perception, some by a certain habituation, and others too in other ways. But each set of principles we must try to investigate in the natural way, and we must take pains to state them definitely, since they have a great influence on what follows. For the beginning is thought to be more than half of the whole, and many of the questions we ask are cleared up by it.

8 We must consider it, however, in the light not only of our conclusion and our premises, but also of what is commonly said about it; for with a true view all the data harmonize, but with a false one the facts soon clash. Now goods have been divided into three classes, and some are described as external, others as relating to soul or to body; we call those that relate to soul most properly and truly goods, and psychical actions and activities we class as relating to soul. Therefore our account must be sound, at least according to this view, which is an old one and agreed on by philosophers. It is correct also in that we identify the end with certain actions and activities; for thus it falls among goods of the soul and not among external goods. Another belief which harmonizes with our account is that the happy man lives well and does well; for we have practically defined happiness as a sort of good

life and good action. The characteristics that are looked for in happiness seem also, all of them, to belong to what we have defined happiness as being. For some identify happiness with virtue, some with practical wisdom, others with a kind of philosophic wisdom, others with these, or one of these, accompanied by pleasure or not without pleasure; while others include also external prosperity. Now some of these views have been held by many men and men of old, others by a few eminent persons; and it is not probable that either of these should be entirely mistaken, but rather that they should be right in at least some one respect or even in most respects.

With those who identify happiness with virtue or some one virtue our account is in harmony; for to virtue belongs virtuous activity. But it makes, perhaps, no small difference whether we place the chief good in possession or in use, in state of mind or in activity. For the state of mind may exist without producing any good result, as in a man who is asleep or in some other way quite inactive, but the activity cannot; for one who has the activity will of necessity be acting, and acting well. And as in the Olympic Games it is not the most beautiful and the strongest that are crowned but those who compete (for it is some of these that are victorious), so those who act win, and rightly win, the noble and good things in life.

Their life is also in itself pleasant. For pleasure is a state of soul, and to each man that which he is said to be a lover of is pleasant; e.g. not only is a horse pleasant to the lover of horses, and a spectacle to the lover of sights, but also in the same way just acts are pleasant to the lover of justice and in general virtuous acts to the lover of virtue. Now for most men their pleasures are in conflict with one another because these are not by nature pleasant, but the lovers of what is noble find pleasant the things that are by nature pleasant; and virtuous actions are such, so that these are pleasant for such men as well as in their own nature. Their life, therefore, has no further need of pleasure as a sort of adventitious charm, but has its pleasure in itself. For, besides what we have said, the man who does not rejoice in noble actions is not even good; since no one would call a man just who did not enjoy acting justly, nor any man liberal who did not enjoy liberal actions; and similarly in all other cases. If this is so, virtuous actions must be in themselves pleasant. But they are also good and noble, and have each of these attributes in the highest degree, since the good man judges well about these attributes; his judgement is such as we have described. Happiness then is the best, noblest, and most pleasant thing in the world, and these attributes are not severed as in the inscription at Delos

Most noble is that which is justest, and best is health;
But pleasantest is it to win what we love.
For all these properties belong to the best activities;
and these, or one – the best – of these, we identify with happiness.

Yet evidently, as we said, it needs the external goods as well; for it is impossible, or not easy, to do noble acts without the proper equipment. In many actions we use friends and riches and political power as instruments; and there are some things the lack of which takes the lustre from happiness, as good birth, goodly children, beauty; for the man who is very ugly in appearance or ill-born or solitary and childless is not very likely to be happy, and perhaps a man would be still less likely if he had thoroughly bad children or friends or had lost good children or friends by death. As we said, then, happiness seems to need this sort of prosperity in addition; for which reason some identify happiness with good fortune, though others identify it with virtue.

9 For this reason also the question is asked, whether happiness is to be acquired by learning or by habituation or some other sort of training, or comes in virtue of some divine providence or again by chance. Now if there is any gift of the gods to men, it is reasonable that happiness should be god-given, and most surely god-given of all human things inasmuch as it is the best. But this question would perhaps be more appropriate to another inquiry; happiness seems, however, even if it is not god-sent but comes as a result of virtue and some process of learning or training, to be among the most godlike things; for that which is the prize and end of virtue seems to be the best thing in the world, and something godlike and blessed.

It will also on this view be very generally shared; for all who are not maimed as regards their potentiality for virtue may win it by a certain kind of study and care. But if it is better to be happy thus than by chance, it is reasonable that the facts should be so, since everything that depends on the action of nature is by nature as good as it can be, and similarly everything that depends on art or any rational cause, and especially if it depends on the best of all causes. To entrust to chance what is greatest and most noble would be a very defective arrangement.

The answer to the question we are asking is plain also from the definition of happiness; for it has been said to be a virtuous activity of soul, of a certain kind. Of the remaining goods, some must necessarily pre-exist as conditions of happiness, and others are naturally co-operative and useful as instruments. And this will be found to agree with what we said at the outset; for we stated the end of political science to be the best end, and political science spends most of its pains on making the citizens to be of a certain character, viz. good and capable of noble acts.

It is natural, then, that we call neither ox nor horse nor any other of the animals happy; for none of them is capable of sharing in such activity. For this reason also a boy is not happy; for he is not yet capable of such acts, owing to his age; and boys who are called happy are being congratulated by reason of the hopes we have for them. For there is required, as we said, not only complete virtue but also a complete life, since many changes occur in life, and all manner of chances, and the most prosperous may fall into great misfortunes in old age, as is told of Priam in the Trojan Cycle; and one who has experienced such chances and has ended wretchedly no one calls happy.

10 Must no one at all, then, be called happy while he lives; must we, as Solon says, see the end? Even if we are to lay down this doctrine, is it also the case that a man is happy when he is dead? Or is not this quite absurd, especially for us who say that happiness is an activity? But if we do not call the dead man happy, and if Solon does not mean this, but that one can then safely call a man blessed as being at last beyond evils and misfortunes, this also affords matter for discussion; for both evil and good are thought to exist for a dead man, as much as for one who is alive but not aware of them; e.g. honours and dishonours and the good or bad fortunes of children and in general of descendants. And this also presents a problem; for though a man has lived happily up to old age and has had a death worthy of his life, many reverses may befall his descendants – some of them may be good and attain the life they deserve, while with others the opposite may be the case; and clearly too the degrees of relationship between them and their ancestors may vary indefinitely. It would be odd, then, if the dead man were to share in these changes and become at one time happy, at another wretched; while it would also be odd if the fortunes of the descendants did not for some time have some effect on the happiness of their ancestors.

But we must return to our first difficulty; for perhaps by a consideration of it our present problem might be solved. Now if we must see the end and only then call a man happy, not as being happy but as having been so before, surely this is a paradox, that when he is happy the attribute that belongs to him is not to be truly predicated of him because we do not wish to call living men happy, on account of the changes that may befall them, and because we have assumed happiness to be something permanent and by no means easily changed, while a single man may suffer many turns of fortune's wheel. For clearly if we were to keep pace with his fortunes, we should often call the same man happy and again wretched, making the happy man out to be chameleon and insecurely based. Or is this keeping pace with his fortunes quite wrong? Success or failure in life does not depend on these, but human life, as we said, needs these as mere additions, while virtuous activities or their opposites are what constitute happiness or the reverse.

The question we have now discussed confirms our definition. For no function of man has so much permanence as virtuous activities (these are thought to be more durable even than knowledge of the sciences), and of these themselves the most valuable are more durable because those who are happy spend their life most readily and most continuously in these; for this seems to be the reason why we do not forget them. The attribute in question, then, will belong to the happy man, and he will be happy throughout his life; for always, or by preference to everything else, he will be engaged in virtuous action and contemplation, and he will bear the chances of life most nobly and altogether decorously, if he is 'truly good' and 'foursquare beyond reproach'.

Now many events happen by chance, and events differing in importance; small pieces of good fortune or of its opposite clearly do not weigh down the scales of life one way or the other, but a multitude of great events if they turn out well will make life happier (for not only are they themselves such as to add beauty to life, but the way a man deals with them may be noble and good), while if they turn out ill they crush and maim happiness; for they both bring pain with them and hinder many activities. Yet even in these nobility shines through, when a man bears with resignation many great misfortunes, not through insensibility to pain but through nobility and greatness of soul.

If activities are, as we said, what gives life its character, no happy man can become miserable; for he will never do the acts that are hateful and mean. For the man who is truly good and wise, we think, bears all the chances life becomingly and always makes the best of circumstances, as a good general makes the best military use of the army at his command and a good shoemaker makes the best shoes out of the hides that are given him; and so with all other craftsmen. And if this is the case, the happy man can never become miserable; though he will not reach blessedness, if he meet with fortunes like those of Priam.

Nor, again, is he many-coloured and changeable; for neither will he be moved from his happy state easily or by any ordinary misadventures, but only by many great ones, nor, if he has had many great misadventures, will he recover his happiness in a short time, but if at all, only in a long and complete one in which he has attained many splendid successes.

When then should we not say that he is happy who is active in accordance with complete virtue and is sufficiently equipped with external goods, not for some chance period but throughout a complete life? Or must we add 'and who is destined to live thus and die as befits his life'? Certainly the future is obscure to us, while happiness, we claim, is an end and something in every way final. If so, we shall call happy those among living men in whom these conditions are, and are to be, fulfilled – but happy men. So much for these questions.

11 That the fortunes of descendants and of all a man's friends should not affect his happiness at all seems a very unfriendly doctrine, and one opposed to the opinions men hold; but since the events that happen are numerous and admit of all sorts of difference, and some come more near to us and others less so, it seems a long – nay, an infinite – task to discuss each in detail; a general outline will perhaps suffice. If, then, as some of a man's own misadventures have a certain weight and influence on life while others are, as it were, lighter, so too there are differences among the misadventures of our friends taken as a whole, and it makes a difference whether the various suffering befall the living or the dead (much more even than whether lawless and terrible deeds are presupposed in a tragedy or done on the stage), this difference also must be taken into account; or rather, perhaps, the fact that doubt is felt whether the dead share in any good or evil. For it seems, from these considerations, that even if anything whether good or evil penetrates to them, it must be something weak and negligible, either in itself or for them, or if not, at least it must be such in degree and kind as not to make happy those who are not happy nor to take away their blessedness from those who are. The good or bad fortunes of friends, then, seem to have some effects on the dead, but effects of such a kind and degree as neither to make the happy unhappy nor to produce any other change of the kind.

12 These questions having been definitely answered, let us consider whether happiness is among the things that are praised or rather among the things that are prized; for clearly it is not to be placed among potentialities. Everything that is praised seems to be praised because it is of a certain kind and is related somehow to something else; for we praise the just or brave man and in general both the good man and virtue itself because of the actions and functions involved, and we praise the strong man, the good runner, and so on, because he is of a certain kind and is related in a certain way to something good and important. This is clear also from the praises of the gods; for it seems absurd that the gods should be referred to our standard, but

this is done because praise involves a reference, to something else. But if if praise is for things such as we have described, clearly what applies to the best things is not praise, but something greater and better, as is indeed obvious; for what we do to the gods and the most godlike of men is to call them blessed and happy. And so too with good things; no one praises happiness as he does justice, but rather calls it blessed, as being something more divine and better.

Eudoxus also seems to have been right in his method of advocating the supremacy of pleasure; he thought that the fact that, though a good, it is not praised indicated it to be better than the things that are praised, and that this is what God and the good are; for by reference to these all other things are judged. Praise is appropriate to virtue, for as a result of virtue men tend to do noble deeds, but encomia are bestowed on acts, whether of the body or of the soul. But perhaps nicety in these matters is more proper to those who have made a study of encomia; to us it is clear from what has been said that happiness is among the things that are prized and perfect. It seems to be so also from the fact that it is a first principle; for it is for the sake of this that we all do all that we do, and the first principle and cause of goods is, we claim, something prized and divine.

13 Since happiness is an activity of soul in accordance with perfect virtue, we must consider the nature of virtue; for perhaps we shall thus see better the nature of happiness. The true student of politics, too, is thought to have studied virtue above all things; for he wishes to make his fellow citizens good and obedient to the laws. As an example of this we have the lawgivers of the Cretans and the Spartans, and any others of the kind that there may have been. And if this inquiry belongs to political science, clearly the pursuit of it will be in accordance with our original plan. But clearly the virtue we must study is human virtue; for the good we were seeking was human good and the happiness human happiness. By human virtue we mean not that of the body but that of the soul; and happiness also we call an activity of soul. But if this is so, clearly the student of politics must know somehow the facts about soul, as the man who is to heal the eyes or the body as a whole must know about the eyes or the body; and all the more since politics is more prized and better than medicine; but even among doctors the best educated spend much labour on acquiring knowledge of the body. The student of politics, then, must study the soul, and must study it with these objects in view, and do so just to the extent which is sufficient for the questions we are discussing; for further precision is perhaps something more laborious than our purposes require.

Some things are said about it, adequately enough, even in the discussions outside our school, and we must use these; e.g. that one element in the soul is irrational and one has a rational principle. Whether these are separated as the parts of the body or of anything divisible are, or are distinct by definition but by nature inseparable, like convex and concave in the circumference of a circle, does not affect the present question.

Of the irrational element one division seems to be widely distributed, and vegetative in its nature, I mean that which causes nutrition and growth; for it is this kind of power of the soul that one must assign to all nurslings and to embryos, and this same power to fullgrown creatures; this is more reasonable than to assign some different power to them. Now the excellence of this seems to be common to all species and not specifically human; for this part or faculty seems to function most in sleep, while goodness and badness are least manifest in sleep (whence comes the saying that the happy are not better off than the wretched for half their lives; and this happens naturally enough, since sleep is an inactivity of the soul in that respect in which it is called good or bad), unless perhaps to a small extent some of the movements actually penetrate to the soul, and in this respect the dreams of good men are better than those of ordinary people. Enough of this subject, however; let us leave the nutritive faculty alone, since it has by its nature no share in human excellence.

There seems to be also another irrational element in the soul-one which in a sense, however, shares in a rational principle. For we praise the rational principle of the continent man and of the incontinent, and the part of their soul that has such a principle, since it urges them aright and towards the best objects; but there is found in them also another element naturally opposed to the rational principle, which fights against and resists that principle. For exactly as paralysed limbs when we intend to move them to the right turn on the contrary to the left, so is it with the soul; the impulses of incontinent people move in contrary directions. But while in the body we see that which moves astray, in the soul we do not. No doubt, however, we must none the less suppose that in the soul too there is something contrary to the rational principle, resisting and opposing it. In what sense it is distinct from the other elements does not concern us. Now even this seems to have a share in a rational principle, as we said; at any rate in the continent man it obeys the rational principle and presumably in the temperate and brave man it is still more obedient; for in him it speaks, on all matters, with the same voice as the rational principle.

Therefore the irrational element also appears to be two-fold. For the vegetative element in no way shares in a rational principle, but the appetitive and in general the desiring element in a sense shares in it, in so far as it listens to and obeys it; this is the sense in which we speak of 'taking account' of one's father or one's friends, not that in which we speak of 'accounting for a mathematical property. That the irrational element is in some sense persuaded by a rational principle is indicated also by the giving of advice and by all reproof and exhortation. And if this element also must be said to have a rational principle, that which has a rational principle (as well as that which has not) will be twofold, one subdivision having it in the strict sense and in itself, and the other having a tendency to obey as one does one's father.

Virtue too is distinguished into kinds in accordance with this difference; for we say that some of the virtues are intellectual and others moral, philosophic wisdom and understanding and practical wisdom being intellectual, liberality and temperance moral. For in speaking about a man's character we do not say that he is wise or has understanding but that he is good-tempered or temperate; yet we praise the wise man also with respect to his state of mind; and of states of mind we call those which merit praise virtues.

Book Two

1 VIRTUE, THEN, BEING OF two kinds, intellectual and moral, intellectual virtue in the main owes both its birth and its growth to teaching (for which reason it requires experience and time), while moral virtue comes about as a result of habit, whence also its name (ethike) is one that is formed by a slight variation from the word ethos (habit). From this it is also plain that none of the moral virtues arises in us by nature; for nothing that exists by nature can form a habit contrary to its nature. For instance the stone which by nature moves downwards cannot be habituated to move upwards, not even if one tries to train it by throwing it up ten thousand times; nor can fire be habituated to move downwards, nor can anything else that by nature behaves in one way be trained to behave in another. Neither by nature, then, nor contrary to nature do the virtues arise in us; rather we are adapted by nature to receive them, and are made perfect by habit.

Again, of all the things that come to us by nature we first acquire the potentiality and later exhibit the activity (this is plain in the case of the senses; for it was not by often seeing or often hearing that we got these senses, but on the contrary we had them before we used them, and did not come to have them by using them); but the virtues we get by first exercising them, as also happens in the case of the arts as well. For the things we have to learn before we can do them, we learn by doing them, e.g. men become builders by building and lyreplayers by playing the lyre; so too we become just by doing just acts, temperate by doing temperate acts, brave by doing brave acts.

This is confirmed by what happens in states; for legislators make the citizens good by forming habits in them, and this is the wish of every legislator, and those who do not effect it miss their mark, and it is in this that a good constitution differs from a bad one.

Again, it is from the same causes and by the same means that every virtue is both produced and destroyed, and similarly every art; for it is from playing the lyre that both good and bad lyre-players are produced. And the corresponding statement is true of builders and of all the rest; men will be good or bad builders as a result of building well or badly. For if this were not so, there would have been no need of a teacher, but all men would have been born good or bad at their craft. This, then, is the case with the virtues also; by doing the acts that we do in our trans- actions with other men we become just or unjust, and by doing the acts that we do in the presence of danger, and being habituated to feel fear or confidence, we become brave or cowardly. The same is true of appetites and feelings of anger; some men become temperate and good-tempered, others self-indulgent and irascible, by behaving in one way or the other in the appropriate circumstances. Thus, in one word, states of character arise out of like activities. This is why the activities we exhibit must be of a certain kind; it is because the states of character correspond to the dif- ferences between these. It makes no small difference, then, whether we form habits of one kind or of another from our very youth; it makes a very great difference, or rather all the difference.

2 Since, then, the present inquiry does not aim at theoretical knowl- edge like the others (for we are inquiring not in order to know what vir- tue is, but in order to become good, since otherwise our inquiry would have been of no use), we must examine the nature of actions, namely how we ought to do them; for these determine also the nature of the states of character that are produced, as we have said. Now, that we must act ac- cording to the right rule is a common principle and must be assumed-it will be discussed later, i.e. both what the right rule is, and how it is related to the other virtues. But this must be agreed upon beforehand, that the whole account of matters of conduct must be given in outline and not precisely, as we said at the very beginning that the accounts we demand must be in accordance with the subject-matter; matters concerned with conduct and questions of what is good for us have no fixity, any more than matters of health. The general account being of this nature, the ac- count of particular cases is yet more lacking in exactness; for they do not fall under any art or precept but the agents themselves must in each case consider what is appropriate to the occasion, as happens also in the art of medicine or of navigation.

But though our present account is of this nature we must give what help we can. First, then, let us consider this, that it is the nature of such things to be destroyed by defect and excess, as we see in the case of strength and of health (for to gain light on things imperceptible we must use the evidence of sensible things); both excessive and defective exercise destroys the strength, and similarly drink or food which is above or below a certain amount destroys the health, while that which is proportionate both produces and increases and preserves it. So too is it, then, in the case of temperance and courage and the other virtues. For the man who flies from and fears everything and does not stand his ground against anything becomes a coward, and the man who fears nothing at all but goes to meet every danger becomes rash; and similarly the man who indulges in every pleasure and abstains from none becomes self-indulgent, while the man who shuns every pleasure, as boors do, becomes in a way insensible; temperance and courage, then, are destroyed by excess and defect, and preserved by the mean.

But not only are the sources and causes of their origination and growth the same as those of their destruction, but also the sphere of their actualization will be the same; for this is also true of the things which are more evident to sense, e.g. of strength; it is produced by taking much food and undergoing much exertion, and it is the strong man that will be most able to do these things. So too is it with the virtues; by abstaining from pleasures we become temperate, and it is when we have become so that we are most able to abstain from them; and similarly too in the case of courage; for by being habituated to despise things that are terrible and to stand our ground against them we become brave, and it is when we have become so that we shall be most able to stand our ground against them.

3 We must take as a sign of states of character the pleasure or pain that ensues on acts; for the man who abstains from bodily pleasures and delights in this very fact is temperate, while the man who is annoyed at it is self-indulgent, and he who stands his ground against things that are terrible and delights in this or at least is not pained is brave, while the man who is pained is a coward. For moral excellence is concerned with pleasures and pains; it is on account of the pleasure that we do bad things, and on account of the pain that we abstain from noble ones. Hence we ought to have been brought up in a particular way from our very youth, as Plato says, so as both to delight in and to be pained by the things that we ought; for this is the right education.

Again, if the virtues are concerned with actions and passions, and every passion and every action is accompanied by pleasure and pain, for this reason also virtue will be concerned with pleasures and pains. This is indicated also by the fact that punishment is inflicted by these means; for it is a kind of cure, and it is the nature of cures to be effected by contraries.

Again, as we said but lately, every state of soul has a nature relative to and concerned with the kind of things by which it tends to be made worse or better; but it is by reason of pleasures and pains that men become bad, by pursuing and avoiding these – either the pleasures and pains they ought not or when they ought not or as they ought not, or by going wrong in one of the other similar ways that may be distinguished. Hence men even define the virtues as certain states of impassivity and rest; not well, however, because they speak absolutely, and do not say 'as one ought' and 'as one ought not' and 'when one ought or ought not', and the other things that may be added. We assume, then, that this kind of excellence tends to do what is best with regard to pleasures and pains, and vice does the contrary.

The following facts also may show us that virtue and vice are concerned with these same things. There being three objects of choice and three of avoidance, the noble, the advantageous, the pleasant, and their contraries, the base, the injurious, the painful, about all of these the good man tends to go right and the bad man to go wrong, and especially about pleasure; for this is common to the animals, and also it accompanies all objects of choice; for even the noble and the advantageous appear pleasant.

Again, it has grown up with us all from our infancy; this is why it is difficult to rub off this passion, engrained as it is in our life. And we measure even our actions, some of us more and others less, by the rule of pleasure and pain. For this reason, then, our whole inquiry must be about these; for to feel delight and pain rightly or wrongly has no small effect on our actions.

Again, it is harder to fight with pleasure than with anger, to use Heraclitus' phrase', but both art and virtue are always concerned with what is harder; for even the good is better when it is harder. Therefore for this reason also the whole concern both of virtue and of political science is with pleasures and pains; for the man who uses these well will be good, he who uses them badly bad.

That virtue, then, is concerned with pleasures and pains, and that by the acts from which it arises it is both increased and, if they are done differently, destroyed, and that the acts from which it arose are those in which it actualizes itself – let this be taken as said.

4 The question might be asked,; what we mean by saying that we must become just by doing just acts, and temperate by doing temperate acts; for if men do just and temperate acts, they are already just and temperate, exactly as, if they do what is in accordance with the laws of grammar and of music, they are grammarians and musicians.

Or is this not true even of the arts? It is possible to do something that is in accordance with the laws of grammar, either by chance or at the suggestion of another. A man will be a grammarian, then, only when he has both done something grammatical and done it grammatically; and this means doing it in accordance with the grammatical knowledge in himself.

Again, the case of the arts and that of the virtues are not similar; for the products of the arts have their goodness in themselves, so that it is enough that they should have a certain character, but if the acts that are in accordance with the virtues have themselves a certain character it does not follow that they are done justly or temperately. The agent also must be in a certain condition when he does them; in the first place he must have knowledge, secondly he must choose the acts, and choose them for their own sakes, and thirdly his action must proceed from a firm and unchangeable character. These are not reckoned in as conditions of the possession of the arts, except the bare knowledge; but as a condition of the possession of the virtues knowledge has little or no weight, while the other conditions count not for a little but for everything, i.e. the very conditions which result from often doing just and temperate acts.

Actions, then, are called just and temperate when they are such as the just or the temperate man would do; but it is not the man who does these that is just and temperate, but the man who also does them as just and temperate men do them. It is well said, then, that it is by doing just acts that the just man is produced, and by doing temperate acts the temperate man; without doing these no one would have even a prospect of becoming good.

But most people do not do these, but take refuge in theory and think they are being philosophers and will become good in this way, behaving somewhat like patients who listen attentively to their doctors, but do none of the things they are ordered to do. As the latter will not be made well in body by such a course of treatment, the former will not be made well in soul by such a course of philosophy.

5 Next we must consider what virtue is. Since things that are found in the soul are of three kinds – passions, faculties, states of character, virtue must be one of these. By passions I mean appetite, anger, fear, confidence, envy, joy, friendly feeling, hatred, longing, emulation, pity, and in general the feelings that are accompanied by pleasure or pain; by faculties the things in virtue of which we are said to be capable of feeling these, e.g. of becoming angry or being pained or feeling pity; by states of character the things in virtue of which we stand well or badly with reference to the

passions, e.g. with reference to anger we stand badly if we feel it violently or too weakly, and well if we feel it moderately; and similarly with reference to the other passions.

Now neither the virtues nor the vices are passions, because we are not called good or bad on the ground of our passions, but are so called on the ground of our virtues and our vices, and because we are neither praised nor blamed for our passions (for the man who feels fear or anger is not praised, nor is the man who simply feels anger blamed, but the man who feels it in a certain way), but for our virtues and our vices we are praised or blamed.

Again, we feel anger and fear without choice, but the virtues are modes of choice or involve choice. Further, in respect of the passions we are said to be moved, but in respect of the virtues and the vices we are said not to be moved but to be disposed in a particular way.

For these reasons also they are not faculties; for we are neither called good nor bad, nor praised nor blamed, for the simple capacity of feeling the passions; again, we have the faculties by nature, but we are not made good or bad by nature; we have spoken of this before. If, then, the virtues are neither passions nor faculties, all that remains is that they should be states of character.

Thus we have stated what virtue is in respect of its genus.

6 We must, however, not only describe virtue as a state of character, but also say what sort of state it is. We may remark, then, that every virtue or excellence both brings into good condition the thing of which it is the excellence and makes the work of that thing be done well; e.g. the excellence of the eye makes both the eye and its work good; for it is by the excellence of the eye that we see well. Similarly the excellence of the horse makes a horse both good in itself and good at running and at carrying its rider and at awaiting the attack of the enemy. Therefore, if this is true in every case, the virtue of man also will be the state of character which makes a man good and which makes him do his own work well.

How this is to happen we have stated already, but it will be made plain also by the following consideration of the specific nature of virtue. In everything that is continuous and divisible it is possible to take more, less, or an equal amount, and that either in terms of the thing itself or relatively to us; and the equal is an intermediate between excess and defect. By the intermediate in the object I mean that which is equidistant from each of the extremes, which is one and the same for all men; by the intermediate relatively to us that which is neither too much nor too little – and this is not one, nor the same for all. For instance, if ten is many and two is few, six is the intermediate, taken in terms of the object; for it exceeds and is exceeded by an equal amount; this is intermediate according to arithmetical proportion. But the intermediate relatively to us is not to be taken so; if ten pounds are too much for a particular person to eat and two too little, it does not follow that the trainer will order six pounds; for this also is perhaps too much for the person who is to take it, or too little – too little for Milo, too much for the beginner in athletic exercises. The same is true of running and wrestling. Thus a master of any art avoids excess and defect, but seeks the intermediate and chooses this – the intermediate not in the object but relatively to us.

If it is thus, then, that every art does its work well – by looking to the intermediate and judgling its works by this standard (so that we often say of good works of art that it is not possible either to take away or to add anything, implying that excess and defect destroy the goodness of works of art, while the mean preserves it; and good artists, as we say, look to this in their work), and if, further, virtue is more exact and better than any art, as nature also is, then virtue must have the quality of aiming at the intermediate. I mean moral virtue; for it is this that is concerned with passions and actions, and in these there is excess, defect, and the intermediate. For instance, both fear and confidence and appetite and anger and pity and in general pleasure and pain may be felt both too much and too little, and in both cases not well; but to feel them at the right times, with reference to the right objects, towards the right people, with the right motive, and in the right way, is what is both intermediate and best, and this is characteristic of virtue. Similarly with regard to actions also there is excess, defect, and the intermediate. Now virtue is concerned with passions and actions, in which excess is a form of failure, and so is defect, while the intermediate is praised and is a form of success; and being praised and being successful are both characteristics of virtue. Therefore virtue is a kind of mean, since, as we have seen, it aims at what is intermediate.

Again, it is possible to fail in many ways (for evil belongs to the class of the unlimited, as the Pythagoreans conjectured, and good to that of the limited), while to succeed is possible only in one way (for which reason also one is easy and the other difficult – to miss the mark easy, to hit it difficult); for these reasons also, then, excess and defect are characteristic of vice, and the mean of virtue;

For men are good in but one way, but bad in many.

Virtue, then, is a state of character concerned with choice, lying in a mean, i.e. the mean relative to us, this being determined by a rational principle, and by that principle by which the man of practical wisdom would determine it. Now it is a mean between two vices, that which depends on excess and that which depends on defect; and again it is a mean because the vices respectively fall short of or exceed what is right in both passions and actions, while virtue both finds and chooses that which is intermediate. Hence in respect of its substance and the definition which states its essence virtue is a mean, with regard to what is best and right an extreme.

But not every action nor every passion admits of a mean; for some have names that already imply badness, e.g. spite, shamelessness, envy, and in the case of actions adultery, theft, murder; for all of these and suchlike things imply by their names that they are themselves bad, and not the excesses or deficiencies of them. It is not possible, then, ever to be right with regard to them; one must always be wrong. Nor does goodness or badness with regard to such things depend on committing adultery with the right woman, at the right time, and in the right way, but simply to do any of them is to go wrong. It would be equally absurd, then, to expect that in unjust, cowardly, and voluptuous action there should be a mean, an excess, and a deficiency; for at that rate there would be a mean of excess and of deficiency, an excess of excess, and a deficiency of deficiency. But as there is no excess and deficiency of temperance and courage because what is intermediate is in a sense an extreme, so too of the actions we have mentioned there is no mean nor any excess and deficiency, but however they are done they are wrong; for in general there is neither a mean of excess and deficiency, nor excess and deficiency of a mean.

7 We must, however, not only make this general statement, but also apply it to the individual facts. For among statements about conduct those which are general apply more widely, but those which are particular are more genuine, since conduct has to do with individual cases, and our statements must harmonize with the facts in these cases. We may take these cases from our table. With regard to feelings of fear and confidence courage is the mean; of the people who exceed, he who exceeds in fearlessness has no name (many of the states have no name), while the man who exceeds in confidence is rash, and he who exceeds in fear and falls short in confidence is a coward. With regard to pleasures and pains – not all of them, and not so much with regard to the pains – the mean is temperance, the excess self-indulgence. Persons deficient with regard to the pleasures are not often found; hence such persons also have received no name. But let us call them 'insensible'.

With regard to giving and taking of money the mean is liberality, the excess and the defect prodigality and meanness. In these actions people exceed and fall short in contrary ways; the prodigal exceeds in spending and falls short in taking, while the mean man exceeds in taking and falls short in spending. (At present we are giving a mere outline or summary, and are satisfied with this; later these states will be more exactly determined.) With regard to money there are also other dispositions – a mean, magnificence (for the magnificent man differs from the liberal man; the former deals with large sums, the latter with small ones), an excess, tastelessness and vulgarity, and a deficiency, niggardliness; these differ from the states opposed to liberality, and the mode of their difference will be stated later. With regard to honour and dishonour the mean is proper pride, the excess is known as a sort of 'empty vanity', and the deficiency is undue humility; and as we said liberality was related to magnificence, differing from it by dealing with small sums, so there is a state similarly related to proper pride, being concerned with small honours while that is concerned with great. For it is possible to desire honour as one ought, and more than one ought, and less, and the man who exceeds in his desires is called ambitious, the man who falls short unambitious, while the intermediate person has no name. The dispositions also are nameless, except that that of the ambitious man is called ambition. Hence the people who are at the extremes lay claim to the middle place; and we ourselves sometimes call the intermediate person ambitious and sometimes unambitious, and sometimes praise the ambitious man and sometimes the unambitious. The reason of our doing this will be stated in what follows; but now let us speak of the remaining states according to the method which has been indicated.

With regard to anger also there is an excess, a deficiency, and a mean. Although they can scarcely be said to have names, yet since we call the intermediate person good-tempered let us call the mean good temper; of the persons at the extremes let the one who exceeds be called irascible, and his vice irascibility, and the man who falls short an inirascible sort of person, and the deficiency inirascibility.

There are also three other means, which have a certain likeness to one another, but differ from one another: for they are all concerned with intercourse in words and actions, but differ in that one is concerned with truth in this sphere, the other two with pleasantness; and of this one kind is exhibited in giving amusement, the other in all the circumstances of life. We must therefore speak of these too, that we may the better see that in all things the mean is praise-worthy, and the extremes neither praiseworthy nor right, but worthy of blame. Now most of these states also have no names, but we must try, as in the other cases, to invent names ourselves so that we may be clear and easy to follow. With regard to truth, then, the intermediate is a truthful sort of person and the mean may be called truthfulness, while the pretence which exaggerates is boastfulness and the person characterized by it a boaster, and that which understates is mock modesty and the person characterized by it mock-modest. With regard to pleasantness in the giving of amusement the intermediate person is ready-witted and the disposition ready wit, the excess is buffoonery and the person characterized by it a buffoon, while the man who falls short is a sort of boor and his state is boorishness. With regard to the remaining kind of pleasantness, that which is exhibited in life in general, the man who is pleasant in the right way is friendly and the mean is friendliness, while the man who exceeds is an obsequious person if he has no end in view, a flatterer if he is aiming at his own advantage, and the man who falls short and is unpleasant in all circumstances is a quarrelsome and surly sort of person.

There are also means in the passions and concerned with the passions; since shame is not a virtue, and yet praise is extended to the modest man. For even in these matters one man is said to be intermediate, and another to exceed, as for instance the bashful man who is ashamed of everything; while he who falls short or is not ashamed of anything at all is shameless, and the intermediate person is modest. Righteous indignation is a mean between envy and spite, and these states are concerned with the pain and pleasure that are felt at the fortunes of our neighbours; the man who is characterized by righteous indignation is pained at undeserved good fortune, the envious man, going beyond him, is pained at all good fortune, and the spiteful man falls so far short of being pained that he even rejoices. But these states there will be an opportunity of describing elsewhere; with regard to justice, since it has not one simple meaning, we shall, after describing the other states, distinguish its two kinds and say how each of them is a mean; and similarly we shall treat also of the rational virtues.

8 There are three kinds of disposition, then, two of them vices, involving excess and deficiency respectively, and one a virtue, viz. the mean, and all are in a sense opposed to all; for the extreme states are contrary both to the intermediate state and to each other, and the intermediate to the extremes; as the equal is greater relatively to the less, less relatively to the greater, so the middle states are excessive relatively to the deficiencies, deficient relatively to the excesses, both in passions and in actions. For the brave man appears rash relatively to the coward,

and cowardly relatively to the rash man; and similarly the temperate man appears self-indulgent relatively to the insensible man, insensible relatively to the self-indulgent, and the liberal man prodigal relatively to the mean man, mean relatively to the prodigal. Hence also the people at the extremes push the intermediate man each over to the other, and the brave man is called rash by the coward, cowardly by the rash man, and correspondingly in the other cases.

These states being thus opposed to one another, the greatest contrariety is that of the extremes to each other, rather than to the intermediate; for these are further from each other than from the intermediate, as the great is further from the small and the small from the great than both are from the equal. Again, to the intermediate some extremes show a certain likeness, as that of rashness to courage and that of prodigality to liberality; but the extremes show the greatest unlikeness to each other; now contraries are defined as the things that are furthest from each other, so that things that are further apart are more contrary.

To the mean in some cases the deficiency, in some the excess is more opposed; e.g. it is not rashness, which is an excess, but cowardice, which is a deficiency, that is more opposed to courage, and not insensibility, which is a deficiency, but self-indulgence, which is an excess, that is more opposed to temperance. This happens from two reasons, one being drawn from the thing itself; for because one extreme is nearer and liker to the intermediate, we oppose not this but rather its contrary to the intermediate. E.g. since rashness is thought liker and nearer to courage, and cowardice more unlike, we oppose rather the latter to courage; for things that are further from the intermediate are thought more contrary to it. This, then, is one cause, drawn from the thing itself; another is drawn from ourselves; for the things to which we ourselves more naturally tend seem more contrary to the intermediate. For instance, we ourselves tend more naturally to pleasures, and hence are more easily carried away towards self-indulgence than towards propriety. We describe as contrary to the mean, then, rather the directions in which we more often go to great lengths; and therefore self-indulgence, which is an excess, is the more contrary to temperance.

9 That moral virtue is a mean, then, and in what sense it is so, and that it is a mean between two vices, the one involving excess, the other deficiency, and that it is such because its character is to aim at what is intermediate in passions and in actions, has been sufficiently stated. Hence also it is no easy task to be good. For in everything it is no easy task to find the middle, e.g. to find the middle of a circle is not for every one but for him who knows; so, too, any one can get angry – that is easy

– or give or spend money; but to do this to the right person, to the right extent, at the right time, with the right motive, and in the right way, that is not for every one, nor is it easy; wherefore goodness is both rare and laudable and noble.

Hence he who aims at the intermediate must first depart from what is the more contrary to it, as Calypso advises

Hold the ship out beyond that surf and spray.

For of the extremes one is more erroneous, one less so; therefore, since to hit the mean is hard in the extreme, we must as a second best, as people say, take the least of the evils; and this will be done best in the way we describe. But we must consider the things towards which we ourselves also are easily carried away; for some of us tend to one thing, some to another; and this will be recognizable from the pleasure and the pain we feel. We must drag ourselves away to the contrary extreme; for we shall get into the intermediate state by drawing well away from error, as people do in straightening sticks that are bent.

Now in everything the pleasant or pleasure is most to be guarded against; for we do not judge it impartially. We ought, then, to feel towards pleasure as the elders of the people felt towards Helen, and in all circumstances repeat their saying; for if we dismiss pleasure thus we are less likely to go astray. It is by doing this, then, (to sum the matter up) that we shall best be able to hit the mean.

But this is no doubt difficult, and especially in individual cases; for or is not easy to determine both how and with whom and on what provocation and how long one should be angry; for we too sometimes praise those who fall short and call them good-tempered, but sometimes we praise those who get angry and call them manly. The man, however, who deviates little from goodness is not blamed, whether he do so in the direction of the more or of the less, but only the man who deviates more widely; for he does not fail to be noticed. But up to what point and to what extent a man must deviate before he becomes blameworthy it is not easy to determine by reasoning, any more than anything else that is perceived by the senses; such things depend on particular facts, and the decision rests with perception. So much, then, is plain, that the intermediate state is in all things to be praised, but that we must incline sometimes towards the excess, sometimes towards the deficiency; for so shall we most easily hit the mean and what is right.

Book Three

1 SINCE VIRTUE IS CONCERNED with passions and actions, and on voluntary passions and actions praise and blame are bestowed, on those that are involuntary pardon, and sometimes also pity, to distinguish the voluntary and the involuntary is presumably necessary for those who are studying the nature of virtue, and useful also for legislators with a view to the assigning both of honours and of punishments. Those things, then, are thought-involuntary, which take place under compulsion or owing to ignorance; and that is compulsory of which the moving principle is outside, being a principle in which nothing is contributed by the person who is acting or is feeling the passion, e.g. if he were to be carried somewhere by a wind, or by men who had him in their power.

But with regard to the things that are done from fear of greater evils or for some noble object (e.g. if a tyrant were to order one to do something base, having one's parents and children in his power, and if one did the action they were to be saved, but otherwise would be put to death), it may be debated whether such actions are involuntary or voluntary. Something of the sort happens also with regard to the throwing of goods overboard in a storm; for in the abstract no one throws goods away voluntarily, but on condition of its securing the safety of himself and his crew any sensible man does so. Such actions, then, are mixed, but are more like voluntary actions; for they are worthy of choice at the time when they are done, and the end of an action is relative to the occasion. Both the terms, then, 'voluntary' and 'involuntary', must be used with reference to the moment of action. Now the man acts voluntarily; for the principle that moves the instrumental parts of the body in such actions is in him, and the things of which the moving principle is in a man himself are in his power to do or not to do. Such actions, therefore, are voluntary, but in the abstract perhaps involuntary; for no one would choose any such act in itself.

For such actions men are sometimes even praised, when they endure something base or painful in return for great and noble objects gained; in the opposite case they are blamed, since to endure the greatest indignities for no noble end or for a trifling end is the mark of an inferior person. On some actions praise indeed is not bestowed, but pardon is, when one does what he ought not under pressure which overstrains human nature and which no one could withstand. But some acts, perhaps, we cannot be forced to do, but ought rather to face death after the most fearful sufferings; for the things that 'forced' Euripides Alcmaeon to slay his mother seem absurd. It is difficult sometimes to determine what should be chosen at what cost, and what should be endured in return for what gain, and yet more difficult to abide by our decisions; for as a rule what is expected is painful, and what we are forced to do is base, whence praise and blame are bestowed on those who have been compelled or have not.

What sort of acts, then, should be called compulsory? We answer that without qualification actions are so when the cause is in the external circumstances and the agent contributes nothing. But the things that in themselves are involuntary, but now and in return for these gains are worthy of choice, and whose moving principle is in the agent, are in themselves involuntary, but now and in return for these gains voluntary. They are more like voluntary acts; for actions are in the class of particulars, and the particular acts here are voluntary. What sort of things are to be chosen, and in return for what, it is not easy to state; for there are many differences in the particular cases.

But if some one were to say that pleasant and noble objects have a compelling power, forcing us from without, all acts would be for him compulsory; for it is for these objects that all men do everything they do. And those who act under compulsion and unwillingly act with pain, but those who do acts for their pleasantness and nobility do them with pleasure; it is absurd to make external circumstances responsible, and not oneself, as being easily caught by such attractions, and to make oneself responsible for noble acts but the pleasant objects responsible for base acts. The compulsory, then, seems to be that whose moving principle is outside, the person compelled contributing nothing.

Everything that is done by reason of ignorance is not voluntary; it is only what produces pain and repentance that is involuntary. For the man who has done something owing to ignorance, and feels not the least vexation at his action, has not acted voluntarily, since he did not know what he was doing, nor yet involuntarily, since he is not pained. Of people, then, who act by reason of ignorance he who repents is thought an involuntary agent, and the man who does not repent may, since he is different, be called a not voluntary agent; for, since he differs from the other, it is better that he should have a name of his own.

Acting by reason of ignorance seems also to be different from acting in ignorance; for the man who is drunk or in a rage is thought to act as a result not of ignorance but of one of the causes mentioned, yet not knowingly but in ignorance.

Now every wicked man is ignorant of what he ought to do and what he ought to abstain from, and it is by reason of error of this kind that men become unjust and in general bad; but the term 'involuntary' tends to be used not if a man is ignorant of what is to his advantage – for it is not mistaken purpose that causes involuntary action (it leads rather to wickedness), nor ignorance of the universal (for that men are blamed), but ignorance of particulars, i.e. of the circumstances of the action and the objects with which it is concerned. For it is on these that both pity and pardon depend, since the person who is ignorant of any of these acts involuntarily.

Perhaps it is just as well, therefore, to determine their nature and number. A man may be ignorant, then, of who he is, what he is doing, what or whom he is acting on, and sometimes also what (e.g. what instrument) he is doing it with, and to what end (e.g. he may think his act will conduce to some one's safety), and how he is doing it (e.g. whether gently or violently). Now of all of these no one could be ignorant unless he were mad, and evidently also he could not be ignorant of the agent; for how could he not know himself? But of what he is doing a man might be ignorant, as for instance people say 'it slipped out of their mouths as they were speaking', or 'they did not know it was a secret', as Aeschylus said of the mysteries, or a man might say he 'let it go off when he merely wanted to show its working', as the man did with the catapult. Again, one might think one's son was an enemy, as Merope did, or that a pointed spear had a button on it, or that a stone was pumicestone; or one might give a man a draught to save him, and really kill him; or one might want to touch a man, as people do in sparring, and really wound him. The ignorance may relate, then, to any of these things, i.e. of the circumstances of the action, and the man who was ignorant of any of these is thought to have acted involuntarily, and especially if he was ignorant on the most important points; and these are thought to be the circumstances of the action and its end. Further, the doing of an act that is called involuntary in virtue of ignorance of this sort must be painful and involve repentance.

Since that which is done under compulsion or by reason of ignorance is involuntary, the voluntary would seem to be that of which the moving principle is in the agent himself, he being aware of the particular circumstances of the action. Presumably acts done by reason of anger or appetite are not rightly called involuntary. For in the first place, on that showing none of the other animals will act voluntarily, nor will children; and secondly, is it meant that we do not do voluntarily any of the acts that are due to appetite or anger, or that we do the noble acts voluntarily and the base acts involuntarily? Is not this absurd, when one and the same thing is the cause? But it would surely be odd to describe as involuntary the things one ought to desire; and we ought both to be angry at certain things and to have an appetite for certain things, e.g. for health and for learning. Also what is involuntary is thought to be painful, but what is in accordance with appetite is thought to be pleasant. Again, what is the difference in respect of involuntariness between errors committed upon calculation and those committed in anger? Both are to be avoided, but the irrational passions are thought not less human than reason is, and therefore also the actions which proceed from anger or appetite are the man's actions. It would be odd, then, to treat them as involuntary.

2 Both the voluntary and the involuntary having been delimited, we must next discuss choice; for it is thought to be most closely bound up with virtue and to discriminate characters better than actions do.

Choice, then, seems to be voluntary, but not the same thing as the voluntary; the latter extends more widely. For both children and the lower animals share in voluntary action, but not in choice, and acts done on the spur of the moment we describe as voluntary, but not as chosen.

Those who say it is appetite or anger or wish or a kind of opinion do not seem to be right. For choice is not common to irrational creatures as well, but appetite and anger are. Again, the incontinent man acts with appetite, but not with choice; while the continent man on the contrary acts with choice, but not with appetite. Again, appetite is contrary to choice, but not appetite to appetite. Again, appetite relates to the pleasant and the painful, choice neither to the painful nor to the pleasant.

Still less is it anger; for acts due to anger are thought to be less than any others objects of choice.

But neither is it wish, though it seems near to it; for choice cannot relate to impossibles, and if any one said he chose them he would be thought silly; but there may be a wish even for impossibles, e.g. for immortality. And wish may relate to things that could in no way be brought about by one's own efforts, e.g. that a particular actor or athlete should win in a competition; but no one chooses such things, but only the things that he thinks could be brought about by his own efforts. Again, wish relates rather to the end, choice to the means; for instance, we wish to be healthy, but we choose the acts which will make us healthy, and we wish to be happy and say we do, but we cannot well say we choose to be so; for, in general, choice seems to relate to the things that are in our own power.

For this reason, too, it cannot be opinion; for opinion is thought to relate to all kinds of things, no less to eternal things and impossible things than to things in our own power; and it is distinguished by its falsity or truth, not by its badness or goodness, while choice is distinguished rather by these.

Now with opinion in general perhaps no one even says it is identical. But it is not identical even with any kind of opinion; for by choosing what is good or bad we are men of a certain character, which we are not by holding certain opinions. And we choose to get or avoid something good or bad, but we have opinions about what a thing is or whom it is good for or how it is good for him; we can hardly be said to opine to get or avoid anything. And choice is praised for being related to the right object rather than for being rightly related to it, opinion for being truly related to its object. And we choose what we best know to be good, but we opine what we do not quite know; and it is not the same people that are thought to make the best choices and to have the best opinions, but some are thought to have fairly good opinions, but by reason of vice to choose what they should not. If opinion precedes choice or accompanies it, that makes no difference; for it is not this that we are considering, but whether it is identical with some kind of opinion.

What, then, or what kind of thing is it, since it is none of the things we have mentioned? It seems to be voluntary, but not all that is voluntary to be an object of choice. Is it, then, what has been decided on by previous deliberation? At any rate choice involves a rational principle and thought. Even the name seems to suggest that it is what is chosen before other things.

3 Do we deliberate about everything, and is everything a possible subject of deliberation, or is deliberation impossible about some things? We ought presumably to call not what a fool or a madman would deliberate about, but what a sensible man would deliberate about, a subject of deliberation. Now about eternal things no one deliberates, e.g. about the material universe or the incommensurability

of the diagonal and the side of a square. But no more do we deliberate about the things that involve movement but always happen in the same way, whether of necessity or by nature or from any other cause, e.g. the solstices and the risings of the stars; nor about things that happen now in one way, now in another, e.g. droughts and rains; nor about chance events, like the finding of treasure. But we do not deliberate even about all human affairs; for instance, no Spartan deliberates about the best constitution for the Scythians. For none of these things can be brought about by our own efforts.

We deliberate about things that are in our power and can be done; and these are in fact what is left. For nature, necessity, and chance are thought to be causes, and also reason and everything that depends on man. Now every class of men deliberates about the things that can be done by their own efforts. And in the case of exact and self-contained sciences there is no deliberation, e.g. about the letters of the alphabet (for we have no doubt how they should be written); but the things that are brought about by our own efforts, but not always in the same way, are the things about which we deliberate, e.g. questions of medical treatment or of money-making. And we do so more in the case of the art of navigation than in that of gymnastics, inasmuch as it has been less exactly worked out, and again about other things in the same ratio, and more also in the case of the arts than in that of the sciences; for we have more doubt about the former. Deliberation is concerned with things that happen in a certain way for the most part, but in which the event is obscure, and with things in which it is indeterminate. We call in others to aid us in deliberation on important questions, distrusting ourselves as not being equal to deciding.

We deliberate not about ends but about means. For a doctor does not deliberate whether he shall heal, nor an orator whether he shall persuade, nor a statesman whether he shall produce law and order, nor does any one else deliberate about his end. They assume the end and consider how and by what means it is to be attained; and if it seems to be produced by several means they consider by which it is most easily and best produced, while if it is achieved by one only they consider how it will be achieved by this and by what means this will be achieved, till they come to the first cause, which in the order of discovery is last. For the person who deliberates seems to investigate and analyse in the way described as though he were analysing a geometrical construction (not all investigation appears to be deliberation – for instance mathematical investigations – but all deliberation is investigation), and what is last in the order of analysis seems to be first in the order of becoming. And if we come on an impossibility, we give up the search, e.g. if we need money and this cannot be got; but if a thing appears possible we try to do it. By 'possible' things I mean things that might be brought about by our own efforts; and these in a sense include things that can be brought about by the efforts of our friends, since the moving principle is in ourselves. The subject of investigation is sometimes the instruments, sometimes the use of them; and similarly in the other cases – sometimes the means, sometimes the mode of using it or the means of bringing it about. It seems, then, as has been said, that man is a moving principle of actions; now deliberation is about the things to be done by the agent himself, and actions are for the sake of things other than themselves. For the end cannot be a subject of deliberation, but only the means; nor indeed can the particular facts be a subject of it, as whether this is bread or has been baked as it should; for these are matters of perception. If we are to be always deliberating, we shall have to go on to infinity.

The same thing is deliberated upon and is chosen, except that the object of choice is already determinate, since it is that which has been decided upon as a result of deliberation that is the object of choice. For every one ceases to inquire how he is to act when he has brought the moving principle back to himself and to the ruling part of himself; for this is what chooses. This is plain also from the ancient constitutions, which Homer represented; for the kings announced their choices to the people. The object of choice being one of the things in our own power which is desired after deliberation, choice will be deliberate desire of things in our own power; for when we have decided as a result of deliberation, we desire in accordance with our deliberation.

We may take it, then, that we have described choice in outline, and stated the nature of its objects and the fact that it is concerned with means.

4 That wish is for the end has already been stated; some think it is for the good, others for the apparent good. Now those who say that the good is the object of wish must admit in consequence that that which the man who does not choose aright wishes for is not an object of wish (for if it is to be so, it must also be good; but it was, if it so happened, bad); while those who say the apparent good is the object of wish must admit that there is no natural object of wish, but only what seems good to each man. Now different things appear good to different people, and, if it so happens, even contrary things.

If these consequences are unpleasing, are we to say that absolutely and in truth the good is the object of wish, but for each person the apparent